thrive PRINCIPLES

thrive
PRINCIPLES

15 Strategies For Building
Your Thriving Life

Lee H. Baucom, Ph.D

New York

thrive PRINCIPLES
15 Strategies For Building Your Thriving Life

Published in New York, New York, by Morgan James Publishing. Morgan James and The Entrepreneurial Publisher are trademarks of Morgan James, LLC. www.MorganJamesPublishing.com

The Morgan James Speakers Group can bring authors to your live event. For more information or to book an event visit The Morgan James Speakers Group at www.TheMorganJamesSpeakersGroup.com.

ISBN 978-1-68350-077-3 paperback
ISBN 978-1-68350-078-0 eBook
ISBN 978-1-68350-079-7 hardcover
Library of Congress Control Number:
2016907705

Cover Design by:
Rachel Lopez
www.r2cdesign.com

Interior Design by:
Bonnie Bushman
The Whole Caboodle Graphic Design

Shelfie

A **free** eBook edition is available
with the purchase of this print book.

CLEARLY PRINT YOUR NAME ABOVE IN UPPER CASE

Instructions to claim your free eBook edition:
1. Download the Shelfie app for Android or iOS
2. Write your name in **UPPER CASE** above
3. Use the Shelfie app to submit a photo
4. Download your eBook to any device

In an effort to support local communities, raise awareness and funds, Morgan James Publishing donates a percentage of all book sales for the life of each book to Habitat for Humanity Peninsula and Greater Williamsburg.

Get involved today! Visit
www.MorganJamesBuilds.com

For Kathy.
Thank you for journeying with me.
For Maggie and Harrison.
Thank you for being a part of the ride.

table of contents

introduction

When John entered my office, his demeanor told me tons. His shoulders were hunched as if he carried the weight of the world. His eyes sagged. He looked like he was dragging himself in.

John plopped down on my couch (yes, I know the stereotype) and began to try and tell me why he was there.

He stumbled around, stammering and looking for the right words. Finally, he said, "I just want to be happy."

It would seem that our culture has joined with John. We all seem to be caught in the elusive search for happiness. The self-help shelves are sagging with the weight of book after book on "how to be happy." And guru after expert is offering advice on how to get there—to that elusive place of endless happiness.

There is only one problem: we are aiming at the wrong target. If you chase happiness, it always seems to stay just out of reach, just like success. One of my favorite authors, Viktor Frankl, said:

"Don't aim at success—the more you aim at it and make it a target, the more you are going to miss it. For success, like happiness, cannot be pursued; it must ensue, and it only does so as the unintended side effect of one's personal dedication to a cause greater than oneself . . . Happiness must happen . . . ."

Happiness is the wrong target. It is a nice side effect, for sure. But it is not the primary target. John is probably a lot like you and me. In reality, he was not so much wanting to be happy. He just didn't want to be unhappy.

If not happiness, what is it that we are aiming for? I believe the primary target is thriving. That is something you *can* aim for, something you can move toward. Happiness is a fleeting emotion. Thriving is a choice. It is a way you build your life.

Thriveology, the study of thriving, is an applied science. It isn't just about facts or understandings, but about application. It's not about knowing how to thrive. It is about regularly taking the steps required to thrive.

In 2003, Paul Pearsall made a passing comment in his book, *The Beethoven Factor*, that there needed to be a curriculum, a framework for how to thrive, a "thrive-ology," he said.

That clicked for me. It encompassed what I had been studying and working toward. It moved beyond what I was seeing and what I was learning, toward how to truly thrive.

Thriving is not based upon what happens to you. It is about how you can choose to live, in spite of what life throws your way. Thriving is about taking on life full-contact—as it is—and growing *through* the challenges.

This is a bit different from our typical response to life events. When Rich came into my office, he told me his desire was to live a "stress-free life." He wanted to insulate himself from stressful events. And so, he wasn't particularly thrilled when I said, "That won't happen. I can't help with that."

Surprised, Rich asked why. I told him, "Because life happens, no matter what. Good things, bad things. They just happen. People come into your life and leave your life. That is part of life. And at the end, you are going to die. That is life."

Rich didn't seem overly thrilled with my diagnosis of life, but was willing to come back. He and I set out to redo some assumptions he had about life. And then we set out to equip him to not just deal with life, but to thrive through life. That is my goal for all the clients who choose to work with me.

How This Book Can Help

Think of this as a curriculum of how to live a thriving life. It is not just about how to live. You can do that. You can hold on, grit your teeth, and grind the days off, one by one. The days, months, and years will pass. And down the road, you can look up with the question, "What was *that* about?"

Or you can take a step beyond that and decide to live a thriving life—fully conscious, with you taking full responsibility. This book is about that latter option.

At the core of this book are 15 principles (divided by chapters), each giving you a tool and a skill for thriving. Each is somewhat independent of the others. And yet, every principle builds when added to the others. They stand alone, but multiply the effect in combination.

As you read, you may find that you have one of several different reactions. First, you may read a chapter and realize you are already aligned with that principle. If you feel that way, you can pat yourself on the back and continue to build your thriving life.

You may read a chapter and have an immediate "wake up moment," where you see the direction and opt to move toward it. You find yourself building a thriving life.

Or you may have a strong negative reaction, convinced that I am wrong, my principle is useless, and this book was a waste. You may hold to that position. But just for a moment, I would ask this: Is your life where you want it to be? Are you thriving? Do you want more?

If your life is not quite where you want it, and you do want to thrive—you do want more—might I suggest you give it a shot? Try out the principle. Give it a bit of time, and see if applying it makes a difference. If not, decide these principles just may not get you where you want to be, and move on. But if you can see a difference, perhaps you might dig in a bit more, just to see if the principles work for you, as they have for so many others.

Let me be clear: many of these ideas are not mine (or at least not mine alone). Principles of thriving have been around for millennia, even if not pulled together and seen as a way to thrive. I am simply pulling together ideas I have studied, bringing them together as a model for how to thrive, and offering them to you as a laboratory of learning. Let's see if they work for you, too.

How To Use This Book

This book is for you to use. It is the culmination of my study, to this point, on how to build a thriving life. I have used these principles as a therapist and a life coach, and applied them in my own life, to build a thriving life. The information is here for you to use, in any way that works for you.

You can think of the book like a video game's design. In the early days of video games (about the last time I played them, so like in Mario Brothers), on each level, you learned skills or gained tools. You would pick up weapons, shields, or powers. Then, you could use those tools to beat the bad guys and do better on the next level.

You can start at the beginning of the book and move through the book to the end. Each principle builds on the previous. And as you add the principles together, their power multiplies.

In more recent games, the ones I watch my son play, you can "free roam" all around the landscape. You can take on a challenge when you want, not necessarily in any order.

So, you can do the same with this book. You can skip around and read what interests you, applying the principles that catch your attention.

One warning: just like in the video games, you may find you are lacking in a weapon or skill, and you have to go back to "catch up," so you can beat the next enemy. If you can't quite make sense of a principle, step back to the prior principles and see if that helps you with the skills you need in order to understand the one you want to master.

And to help you with that, I include a little cheat at the end of each chapter. In Internet parlance, if I were to send you a long article, too long for you to likely read, I might mark the message with *TL;DR*. That means, "Too Long, Don't/ Didn't Read," followed with a short synopsis of the information.

In Thriveology, each chapter ends with a one-page TL;DR page, telling you the minimum you need to know in order to understand the chapter. You can use that as a review of each chapter to make sure you understand the key points. Or you can use it as the quick summary to help you understand another principle or chapter.

One More Note

There is nothing deeply complicated in learning to thrive. No esoteric knowledge. No "magic bullet" that turns it all around. No incantation that will suddenly make your life bulletproof and without issues. We tend to complicate things too much. Usually, the best approach is the simple and direct approach.

In fact, the struggles and problems in life are what give you the fuel to build a stronger, more thriving life. They become the underpinnings of your stronger, more resilient self. This is something we know, but promptly forget. How do you build a muscle? Stress it by making it lift more than it did before (give it a challenge). The muscle rises to the challenge. Or how do you learn any task you don't already know? By doing it, failing, refining, and continuing until you succeed. In other words, you challenge yourself.

This is important, though: the real trick is application. Many people spend their time studying, researching, and looking for the answers. They spend little time in application, the "doing" of life.

These principles are meant to give you a method of doing. They are designed to help you take on life. The goal is not to defeat it, but to use whatever happens, whatever challenges or difficulties, successes and victories, to build a thriving life.

That is much better than chasing after happiness. And much deeper. (And within your control.)

So, let's go build a thriving life!

Chapter 1

time to thrive

Life happens. No matter what you or I do, life just happens. There are high moments and low moments, easy times and tough times. There are pains and hurts, joys and achievements. That's just life.

How do you live through what life gives you? That is the question.

You can pass through life, barely hanging on, scraping by, basically surviving. You can fight and fuss, believe that life just isn't fair, and see yourself as a victim. And you will exhaust yourself in a losing battle.

Or you can pass through, oblivious to what is happening, more or less assuming that life will get started at some point. Your "cruise control" is set and you are just passing through. And one day, you wake up and ask, "Where did life go?"

Or, you can go through life fulfilled and excited. You can live life with a purpose and a deep sense of meaning, impacting lives all around. In other words, you can live a thriving life.

Here's the interesting thing: what happens to you is not the difference in those three trajectories. How you understand yourself and life, and how you respond to those life events—that is what makes the difference.

Having nothing or having too much is not the determining issue. Many people, barely scraping by (materially speaking), live thriving lives. And many people, with more than enough, feel like they are barely surviving.

My friend John, whom you met in the Introduction, was in survival mode. He firmly believed that life had dealt him a bad hand. I heard, "Life isn't fair," way too many times.

John pulled into my parking lot in a very expensive car, stepped out dressed in very nice clothes, coming from the business he owned.

"Life not fair"? John was correct. Life was not fair to him. But he saw it from the wrong end. He had a winning hand. He just didn't see it. He lived in "survival mode," but only in his mind.

John struggled every day, but mostly with himself. He had no idea that he had life by the horns, and not the other way around. His belief was focused on a lack of something every day. The "something" might change, but the feeling of lack stayed the same.

Sue, on the other hand, was someone I met during my years as a hospital chaplain. She was a frequent patient on the floor I covered, the oncology floor. Sue had been diagnosed with metastatic breast cancer two years earlier. The same week she was diagnosed with cancer, her husband told her he was leaving her for another woman.

In the dark evenings of our visits (I covered the second shift, a quiet time in the hospital), Sue and I chatted. She told me her story early on. "Wow," I thought, "I bet she is bitter."

Sue was facing the end of her life. The radiation and chemotherapy only partially beat back the cancer from her post-operative body. It was never defeated. She had fought and fought, but the cancer was relentless.

Over the course of those couple of years, I saw Sue many times. And I kept waiting for the bitterness and anger.

One night, I ventured, "Do you ever just feel that life is unfair?"

"Oh, God, yes!" Sue told me.

Finally, I thought, here comes the anger.

Then Sue continued, "Life is definitely unfair. I have had more than my share of joy. I have had more than my share of opportunities. And I have had more than my share of love. Life is definitely unfair . . . in my favor!"

Sue shared that she had once felt the equation was tilted the other way. She thought that she was on the losing end. I asked her what woke her up. "Cancer," she told me.

She explained that she had been going through life, angry and upset. She tried to control others in her life, and tried to control her own life. But to no avail. Other people still did what they wanted, and she always felt out of control.

Then, along came cancer. "It woke me up," she told me. She said she realized, while waiting for surgery, that no matter what happened, cancer would not beat her. She took on the challenge, not to get well and live forever, but to live well while she was alive.

While many in a similar spot might bargain with God (or some higher power), Sue decided that she would live life as fully as possible. She was not trying to escape death, but live life.

Sue made a choice to thrive.

And that is the nature of thriving—it is about making a choice to thrive. It is about not numbing out and living on automatic. It is about living fully.

Surviving Versus Thriving

John was stuck in survival mode. Sue had shifted to "thrival mode." She had become a thriver.

The difference was not about what "stuff" either had, or even differences in living a "charmed life." John was in good health. Sue was at the end of her life.

But there were differences. For example, there was a difference in mindset. John believed he had somehow been done wrong. So he looked at every event through that lens. Sue, on the other hand, had a mindset that life was precious and she needed to make the most of what she had. It was a difference in seeing lack or in seeing abundance.

John believed he had no choices in life. He was stuck. Sue believed she always had a choice, which allowed her to move through life with intentionality.

And since John believed he had no choices, he would not see any intentionality possible on his part.

Sue was about growth. John was about being stuck. And that is key: survival mode is about "staying the same," in spite of the frustration of just holding on. Thrival mode is about changing, even if the only change possible is in one's own perspective.

Surviving is based in fear. Fears hold you tight, telling you what you don't have, can't do, and shouldn't do.

Thriving is about aspirations: what you want to move toward, who you want to be, and how you will live your life.

Thriving is a move toward meaning and purpose. It is about taking responsibility and raising your own personal standards.

(We will talk about all of this in more detail in later chapters.)

How I Got Here

In 2002, I got sick. Very sick. I remember overhearing a discussion between my wife and my doctor on the phone. My doctor was telling my wife there was an 86% chance that I would be permanently disabled. Eventually, the doctor believed, I would die from my illness.

That was a big wake-up call. Well, the "wake-up" actually came a bit later. First, I had to struggle through several months of feeling horrible, tired, and defeated. I simply dragged myself (quite literally) through the day. Morning came, and I stumbled through the day, trying to do whatever work I could. Evening came, and I promptly fell asleep, reliving it over and over, like the movie Groundhog Day.

But I was fortunate. I started to recover. I am not disabled, and have, as of yet, not died. My body got the upper hand. The doctor's diagnosis was correct, but his prognosis was wrong.

When I got better, I woke up. I realized that, although I study resilience, I was not thriving.

Let me back up just a bit.

During college, I was trying to decide what I would do with my life. My wise mother asked me what others came to me for, how I naturally worked in the world. It was a great question. She was asking a question about passion and potential: what did I love doing, and what was I good at?

People always came to me for advice and assistance, support and guidance. It never really occurred to me, but I was already doing what I wanted to do: I was helping people live a better life.

My initial understanding of that "calling" was to be a therapist. Originally, I thought I would pursue a career as a Marriage and Family Therapist. This changed to the ministry of Pastoral Counseling. So, off to graduate school I went to gain training as a Pastoral Counselor. Two masters and a Ph.D. later, I was headed toward that career path.

But there are a couple of other important details. First, during my graduate school training, I began to have misgivings about the theories and approaches to helping people that I was being taught. I began to question the underpinnings of psychotherapy and family therapy. Throughout my graduate studies, I raised questions and searched for the answers to the problems. Over time, I grew more and more disenchanted with the pathology orientation of therapy. "What about the up side of life?" I kept wondering. We were always focused on the downside, but not on how to help people get to the upside.

Second, as I was finishing up my dissertation, I read an article about Life Coaching. This was the early days of "life coaching." When I read the description, I turned to my wife and said, "This is how I do counseling." Needless to say, my wife, with a little frustration, given the years devoted to my studies, asked, "So, what are you going to do about it?"

I completed my dissertation, graduated, and started a three-year coach-training program one month later. That was in 1996.

My reading had already shifted during graduate school, but I began to really seek out positive psychology, resilience, and growth theory studies.

How was it, I wondered, that people could rise *above* the hurts and struggles in life? How could people live a full, meaningful, purposeful life despite the hardships they'd encountered?

I never doubted that people suffered through life. I had just lost faith that therapy did much to actually eliminate the suffering. In fact, in many ways, it seemed that therapy had the potential of keeping someone stuck in their suffering.

Sigmund Freud, arguably the father of modern psychotherapy, even stated that the goal of psychoanalysis was to move from neurosis to "common, ordinary unhappiness." Perhaps Freud was having a bad day, but that is not a lofty goal.

I began to see that people really could live above the old hurts and wounds. People could discover a deeper meaning, make a greater impact, and live a higher life. I began to see that life was not about solving your problems and making it to zero, but about moving into the positive. In fact, I now see that those issues that "held us back" are the fuel to "propel you forward."

Let me be clear: I don't make a claim that I am thriving in all areas of my life all the time. I do claim that I keep learning and growing, moving toward more thriving. My current business card probably says it all. It states I am a full-time Thriveologist (meaning I spend my time learning and teaching the skills of thriving), but that I am a part-time thriver. Just like everyone else, I struggle to always apply the principles of how to live a full, thriving life. My goal is to close the gap on how to always thrive.

The principles in this book are the same strategies I employ. They have proven invaluable for shifting me from striving and surviving to thriving. I hope you find them useful in *your* building a (more) thriving life!

Chapter 2

a thought is a thought

b y my definition, thriving is about becoming our fullest and ever-better self—actively involved in the world, living an engaged and meaningful life in the present on the way to an even greater future. Ideally, our past serves us as a reservoir of learning and experience that enables us to move forward on our path and to help others do the same.

For most people, however, the past still holds us in its grip. We're caught up replaying and regretting it—over and over and over again—in our minds and often in our daily lives. We focus on what we don't want and don't have rather than on what we do. Our challenge, then, is to orient ourselves in the Here and Now and to find ways to thrive from now on—no matter what.

Moving ahead in life is always a struggle between our fears and aspirations, our doubts and our desires. But these polarities need not result in an internal tug-of-war that brings us to a standstill. Instead, they can work together to propel us in the direction of our dreams.

For instance, some of our fears help us steer clear of dangerous situations. But they can also indicate where it is we actually want to travel—outside the safety of our comfort zone. And while self-doubt can keep us stuck in unsatisfying patterns, our burning desires can motivate us to do what it takes to move beyond them.

As you may have noticed in your own life, the fear of success can be as debilitating as the fear of failure—if we let it stop us. We may be afraid we can't have what we want, that we don't deserve to have it, or any of a number of other self-limiting thoughts. So what a Thriver does to get the upper hand on these crippling beliefs is to remember that a thought is just a thought—the thought is not a Truth and it need not be the rule by which we live.

No doubt you've heard the analogy made between our self-limiting behaviors—based on our false beliefs—and how a powerful elephant can be tethered to a flimsy stick by a thin rope because it was conditioned as a baby to identify its tether as stronger than it is. Our thoughts are even more flimsy than the rope and stick. Yet, how often do they keep us from escaping our past?

Years ago, when I was studying to become a therapist, I was driven by the desire to help as many people as possible to actualize their greatest potential to create a meaningful life of value, pleasure, and service. To do this, I knew we needed to find a way to harmonize the internal chorus of dissonant voices that often argue us out of effective action.

Since our mind is clearly our most invaluable asset *and* our most formidable stumbling block, I saw that understanding the mind was essential if we wanted to thrive in every circumstance—whether favorable or unfavorable. So, one of the obvious "secrets" I learned along the way is that people who thrive recognize that a thought is really just a thought—a flimsy tether that holds us in place through our own faith in its reality. The only actual power it has is the power we give to it through the potent creative energy of our attention and belief.

Over time, I have discovered that one fundamental mistake we make—and one that continually keeps us from thriving—is believing what our mind is saying. We buy into our thoughts. To be clear, thoughts can be important. But there is one very important thing to remember: a mind is designed to do one thing, create thoughts. Some are helpful. Some are not. The mind doesn't care, as long as it is creating thoughts.

Our task, then, is to understand what the mind does, and stop believing that everything our mind says is a) true, or b) helpful.

Mental Noise Annoys Us All—Until It Doesn't Anymore

It is generally estimated that the mind churns out about 50-80,000 thoughts per day. The majority of these thoughts are automatic, repetitive, pointless, negative, and debilitating—rather than fresh, creative, inspired, insightful, and beneficial. I don't mean to degrade thoughts but just to put them in the right perspective. After all, a thought is just a thought! But what a powerful thing that can be.

The same process of thinking that gets us into trouble can inspire us to do great, creative things in every field of human endeavor. Thoughts are what allow us to accumulate information, develop an understanding of something of interest to us, and turn that understanding into actionable wisdom. Through our thoughts, we can create great beauty or great destruction—if we let them run and ruin our lives.

If you've ever tried to sit quietly without thinking for even a few moments, you'll know how very difficult that is. Thoughts keep popping into our heads, on and on and on—24/7. When people start to meditate, one of the first things they discover is just how noisy their mind really is and how difficult it is to disengage from the endless parade of passing thoughts.

Notice that one of the many benefits people gain from meditation is the recognition that a thought really is just a thought and nothing more than that. Thoughts are like wisps of clouds moving across the sky. They only remain overhead, grow dark, and rain upon us if we empower them to do so through a personal investment of our attention and belief.

In truth, it's not thinking that is the problem. The mind churns thoughts out endlessly and that's okay. That's just what minds do. So, it's up to us how we manage our thoughts.

Left unmanaged, thoughts can lead people into depression and anxiety, into addiction, aggression, and ruin. When we forget that a thought is just a thought, they can begin to overtake us. What was just a passing thought a moment ago can become our "big truth" if we allow it to gain emotional momentum and then take action on it.

The problem is not with thinking. I don't think the goal is to have no thoughts in your head (nor do I think that possible). The problem is forgetting we are thinking and confusing the thought with reality. It can seem obvious when we are calm and in a higher mood. But when life is tough and our mood is lower, thoughts take on an apparent reality. The thought is confused with the real (and many times, we end up turning that thought into our reality).

Fighting With Ourselves

Have you (or someone you know) ever made up a story about what someone else is thinking, believing, or intending to do—and then had a big reaction to it? Actually, it's a fairly common pastime. We make assumptions about the meaning of another person's glances, gestures, words, and actions, which then precipitates a cascade of turbulent thoughts, emotions, and beliefs in us.

Yet, in all that "much ado about nothing," we may never have touched on truth. We may simply have been the "victim" of a painful drama that we ourselves write in our own minds. We take the fiction of our mind and turn it into non-fiction in our lives.

A friend of mine told me of a time when she was meditating and then dropped, for an instant, into 'twilight sleep'—that space between waking and dreaming. Moments later, when she snapped out of it, she realized that in that subliminal state she'd been involved in a heated argument with several people.

She had been adamant in her conviction about the correctness of the point she'd been arguing with them. But when she came back to consciousness, she realized that the people she was arguing with did not actually exist—nor did the issue she was arguing about. She wasn't rehashing a disagreement she'd recently had with someone she knew. This was a total fabrication that her mind had created, which then triggered her rage—in that brief instant between waking and dreaming. And nothing had happened, other than a thought.

How often do we go through our lives more asleep than awake—making fallacious assumptions about other people as we go and then acting on them? When we forget that those thoughts are just what our mind is automatically producing, we begin to write a story in our own minds and, in an almost trance-like state, live it out. We cause our thoughts to become reality—all because we confused a thought with reality in the first place.

A friend was thinking about the many homeless people she'd seen on street corners loudly ranting at invisible adversaries. She then realized that this isn't just what "crazy people" do. It's what the mind, itself, does when "no one's at home" to evaluate, direct, ignore, and/or quiet it down in moments when it has no useful purpose to serve. That's a primary principle for effective thought understanding and management.

As we become more awake and aware in our daily lives, we also become more rapidly discerning when a troubling thought arises. We're able to determine if it deserves a second look or whether we'd be best served just to let it go.

Someone who is mentally ill may not be able to make the distinction between what they think and what is true. Someone who is thriving is able to say, "Okay. That's not reality; that's just me thinking." And, as a really wise bumper sticker states, "I don't have to believe everything that I think."

Thoughts Lead To Feelings

The way we think about something creates our emotions. If you doubt that this is true, here's a simple experiment to try for a few moments:

1. Focus on a particular emotional state of your choosing. It can be anger or happiness, frustration or contentment, sadness or a feeling of inner freedom and joy. Make yourself feel that chosen emotion. Give yourself a few moments to create that emotion.

2. Once you create that feeling, spend a few moments really focusing on it, turning it around in your mind and tuning into the sensations the thoughts produce in your body. Let yourself dwell there for a few minutes. Consider what it is you are feeling now that you weren't in touch with a few minutes ago before this experience.

3. After you've completed your experiment, make sure to bring yourself back to a neutral space—especially if you chose a difficult feeling. But if you chose a pleasant one, remember the steps you took to get yourself into that good-feeling state and repeat the process often.

4. Now, let me ask you a question: What did you do to get to that emotional state? Did you go in search of a thought about something or someone, a memory or event, that made you feel that way? Did you think back to a time when you had that emotion and focused on what was happening in that moment?

If you are like everyone else who has tried this, you created your emotional state by accessing a thought that made you feel that way. You pulled a thought out of your mind, focused on it, and created an emotion.

As you have just demonstrated to yourself, we have the capacity to make ourselves happy or miserable without a lot of help from anyone else or even from outside circumstances. Happiness and misery are largely an "inside job." Wherever our thoughts and feelings may land us on the emotional spectrum from positive to negative, they attract like thoughts and feelings to them and build from there.

We often do this on a regular basis. Sometimes, these thoughts that really catch our attention come from some deeply held beliefs. But remember that beliefs are just thoughts we think over and over again until they create a groove in our mind to which the mind frequently returns—in the belief that they are true.

A friend of mine is a good example of this. She always believes that people are upset and angry with her. That is her belief, based on a thought she keeps repeating to herself and others. When she interacts with someone, that thought creates a viewpoint. She sees any action as proof of this. Someone looks at her in a certain way, and she is convinced the person is angry. Someone fails to return a phone call, and she believes it to be due to anger. Or someone doesn't do something promised—this is seen as proof of anger.

In reality, people give funny looks, forget to call back, and forget to follow through. Not because of anger or anything else. But because people are distracted and living in their own little worlds.

Instead of seeing this reality, my friend continues to believe that people's inattention is a sign of their anger towards her. Needless to say, she becomes angry or hurt (her emotions) due to those thoughts. Her thought leads to her emotion. And those emotions then lead to her actions towards other people.

Our Own Port in the Storm

Personally, I believe that we are all very powerful creators—whether we know it and desire it or not. We play a leading role in creating our moods and the lives we live. And our beliefs, and the emotions they engender, move out from us in actions that affect those around us. These actions may be tied to thoughts. And those thoughts are just that: thoughts.

Because of this, thrivers actually view what happens to them in the world as a reflection of what's going on inside themselves. They also use it as an opportunity for greater self-awareness and choice about how to respond to "external" events. As a result, blame becomes less and less of an option for those who desire to thrive no matter what. Self-growth is what matters most to them.

This doesn't mean that they have to avoid the lower, heavier emotions. In truth, we can't. They're all part of the experience of being human. But when we're feeling angry, resentful, jealous, or extremely frustrated, it's important to keep in mind that these feelings are, in large part, generated by the thoughts that are rumbling through our heads.

Offering compassion to ourselves as well as to others can help to soothe and calm a troubled heart and release unhappy thoughts and feelings. Quieting the mind—through belly breathing and meditation—can also put us into a more neutral, less reactive state. Then, we're less prone to make up stories about ourselves and other people. You know the stories that I'm talking about—the ones that go like this, "I'm always the one who is overlooked and left out," "I'm the last to know," "No one really loves me," "I'll never be able to do that," "I know she won't go out with me," or "I'll probably screw up this relationship like I did all the others."

Just by noticing our thinking, and becoming a witness to our thoughts and feelings—rather than a full-on participant—we can create a greater sense of awareness that those thoughts are just thoughts. We can also stop the vicious cycle of self-victimization through our negative judgments and thoughts!

It all starts with the awareness that a thought is simply that—a thought. It is not real. It is our thinking about reality. Feelings come from those thoughts. So, while we can't stop the thinking, the less we "buy into" our thoughts, the more our emotional life stays in a positive zone.

How We View the World

Each of us sees the world through a particular lens—our personal belief system or paradigm. This worldview is made up of the thoughts and beliefs we hold, many of which come from the people around us. We naturally assume these are truths about the world in which we live when we are very young. Only later, as we are exposed to a variety of other perspectives, do we recognize that these adopted opinions and suppositions about life and the world are just points of view, not the whole picture.

In addition to these assumed perspectives, our personal paradigm is also composed of the conclusions we have drawn—and unconscious decisions we have made—based on our perceptions and interpretations of the experiences we've had from the time we were born to the present moment. Clearly, the lens through which we view the world is far from 20-20. It has a lot of distortions in it.

Recently, a peace activist told his story on one of NPR's weekend story hours. His father had been his hero when he was a young child. The men who came to visit at their home admired his father greatly and looked to him for leadership. So the young boy grew up believing that his father was a great, heroic man.

Having been born into a racist environment, the boy was surprised to learn at a summer camp that his new best friend was Jewish. He'd never met a Jewish person before but was filled with negative expectations about them, which this boy in no way matched. A few years later—after his father and his father's friends were convicted and imprisoned for murderous terrorist acts —the story-teller came to understand that the paradigm and world view in which he grew up was incomplete and inaccurate.

It's easy to forget that we are living in and seeing through a paradigm that we mistake for reality. We believe our perspective is true and accurate despite how different it may be from someone else's. It's often not until something extraordinary occurs that we discover that the lens through which we've viewed the world is focused in a way that leads to harm.

All of us see through our own often invisible and largely unconscious assumptions about life. If somebody else were to look through your paradigm, the world would look very different than it does through their own—even if you share the same religious and political views.

Think of what it's like when you put on someone else's prescription glasses. Chances are, everything will look kind of weird to you. The fact is, there are as many points of view—or lenses of perception—as there are people on this planet. The problem comes from forgetting that our way of seeing the world is a perspective derived from many influences—rather than an accurate perception of reality.

The fact that we all have a certain perspective, a point of view, is not at all the problem. The problem is that we forget this fact and believe that what we see is, indeed, reality. Not perspective, but reality.

This point was made in a memorable way by the famous Japanese film director, Akira Kurosawa. In his 1950's film, *Rashomon*, a serious crime is committed and each of the participants and witnesses tell a contradictory story about it. The term Rashomon Effect has come to mean "contradictory interpretations of the same event by different people."

The ways we see reality are all influenced by multiple factors that all contain inaccuracies. "Eye witnesses" rarely share the same view. And it doesn't matter if they are witnessing an accident or just watching life go by. Their viewpoints will never match.

H.A.L.T.

When our mood is low, when our energy is down, when we're feeling stressed, defeated and depleted, we're particularly susceptible to seeing events through very dark glasses and mistaking our negative thoughts about them for accurate interpretations of reality. More than that, when our resources are low, we are more likely to forget that our "reality" is just one perspective, incomplete and inaccurate.

That's why people are advised—at 12-Step meetings—to "H.A.L.T." their ceaseless thinking and believing in their thoughts most especially when they're Hungry, Angry, Lonely, and/or Tired. That's when the negative inner chatter can become particularly toxic. That is also when we confuse our personal paradigm with reality.

One of the prominent voices that many hear in their heads—especially when they're under stress—is the "Inner Critic." In some people, it is an ever-present commentator letting them know how far short they have fallen in their efforts, and how much less they are than the people all around them. But whether you have a noisy inner critic and/or a chipper inner coach, it's important to remember that we are all works-in-progress.

What thrivers do so well is to recognize that our thoughts are just part of the noisy stream of consciousness bubbling through our mind. And all of us can make the choice to "pay them no mind." If we do give credence to our thoughts, then they are free to weave a multitude of stories about reality—without ever necessarily touching on truth.

Thoughts are like Lego blocks—one easily attaching to another, then another, and another until we've created an entire fantastical structure that looks real and solid—but doesn't hold much weight. Once people recognize that a thought is just a thought, with no weight or real strength of its own, they usually think that they should control their thoughts. But I say, "good luck with that."

Instead of getting caught in the trap of trying—and failing—to stop our runaway trains of thought in their tracks, we can adopt a thriver's strategy. The first step in that strategy is to recognize and accept that the incessant inner chatter is an automatic process of the mind. There's no need to get upset about it, to try to control it—or to pay a whole lot of attention to it. It's just what the mind does all the time. Some of these thoughts are going to be helpful and can be used to move us forward toward our goals. Some are going to be unhelpful. So the crucial skill to cultivate is discernment.

We don't have to judge our thoughts as "good" or "bad" but rather to see at a glance whether they're helpful or not. Do they improve how we feel, or diminish our sense of self and possibilities? Do they help or hinder us—inspire or defeat us? In a sense, we become the traffic cop—accepting and directing the flow of traffic as it comes at us from all directions.

A helpful thought is still not reality. But it may move you in a more thriving direction. Conversely, rarely is an unhelpful thought rooted in reality. It is, in either case, just a thought. Which one would you want to hold? Which one would you want to release?

Gaining Mastery of the Mind

Have you ever awakened in a fairly good mood—but immediately your mind went searching for what it had been worrying about the night before? Like a dog sniffing around for a choice bone, the mind is not content until it finds the very problem it wants to chew on.

Or perhaps, as soon as you wake up in the morning, your mind starts focusing on all the challenges you're going to have to face that day. And the more you think about them, the less you want to get out of bed because you feel defeated before you've even begun.

If we want to thrive in the midst of the constant challenges life throws our way, then it's important—as soon as we notice one of these negative thoughts building in our mind—that we give it no place to roost. When it comes to halting worrying, here's what thrivers do:

They acknowledge that there may well be difficulties to deal with up ahead.

They accept the uncomfortable feelings they have about that.

They note the thoughts that are creating those feelings, and recognize they are just thoughts. No more true than other thoughts. Just thoughts.

Then, like a good coach, they focus on their strengths and past successes, and on the blessings that they enjoy in this very moment.

And they decide to let the thought go, allowing a thought to do what thoughts do, drift away (when allowed).

After that, they're in a better position to create and focus on an action plan that helps them to deal more effectively with the challenges they're facing. If, instead, we allow ourselves to be scared by the thoughts and fears our minds automatically produce, we'll soon be surrounded by a "thought storm" that threatens to blow us off course.

When under the attack of a thought storm—it may seem that all the messages your mind is generating are truths. But even if the thoughts are somewhat valid in the moment, if they disempower you, they're worse than worthless. And unless and until you turn your thinking into action, a thought is just a thought. And you are meant to serve as the gatekeeper.

Feeling What You're Thinking

Some thoughts pass through our minds in a flash. Something occurs to us in one moment and in the next it's gone. (I find that the ones that seem to slip away the fastest are my good ideas!)

Other thoughts stick around (usually, for me, the less useful thoughts)—especially if we give them credence, mull them over, and fixate on them. Soon, they're occupying major real estate in our mind. Somewhere along the line, we've forgotten how to exercise the choice to release a negative thought and focus elsewhere. Catching the thought earlier in the process can save a lot of time and discomfort.

I love that term, "entertaining a thought." It is too true. In many ways, we are handing energy over to the thought, doing our little "dance steps" of anxiety and making the thought ever more content to stick around and become entrenched.

Those thoughts with negative energy around them (based on our fears and anxieties) are the ones that grab our attention and rivet us to the show. That show, more often than not, is fictitious. It only feels real because we keep entertaining that thought. It is much like a scary movie, where we lose our separation from the movie and begin to feel that we are *in* the movie. But in an instant, you may just remind yourself, "It is only a movie," and find the fear falling away. In the same way, "It is just a thought," gives you the necessary distance from the thought—and the thought can just fall away. The anxiety follows it.

Here's what thrivers do. They stay aware of what they're feeling because emotions are a great barometer of our thoughts. If you find yourself feeling uneasy, stressed or depressed, chances are you've been focusing on a distressing thought. So, here's something essential to keep in mind: The unpleasant feelings may be very strong and convincing. But they are not an accurate indicator of the validity of the thoughts that caused them. All you can measure from these feelings is the impact the thought has upon your feelings.

As we begin to use our emotions as a barometer for our thinking, we become more aware of what's going on inside ourselves at an earlier point in the process. Then, we can choose to drop the thought and let it fall away. After all, we're the ones in charge and it has to follow our lead—when we are consistent in our training.

At the beach house where we vacation, my father has a clock in the hall, which has a barometer in it. When we arrive, I place the marker on the needle's position. From there, I can get a feel for where things are, weather-wise. If I see the needle move upward from the position I marked, I don't worry. We can enjoy the beach, go about our activities and enjoy vacation. Higher pressure marks good weather. I simply don't have to focus on that.

But if the needle drops below my mark, I start thinking about other activities. It might be a good day to shop or head to the movies. Low pressure means some rough weather may be approaching.

So, "barometrically speaking," when your emotions are on the higher side, when you are feeling content, joyful, even happy, you don't need to worry about your thoughts. But, if you are feeling angry, upset, resentful, frustrated, or disappointed, it may just be time to ask, "What am I thinking about?" Notice the thought that led to the "lower pressure" and decide to let it go. Release it. Good weather (and higher feelings) will return.

Evolving the Brain

Sometimes, we find that we have repetitive thoughts. The same ones keep on coming along. They end up forming a thought train. Our "trains of thought" run along old familiar tracks. And over time, these tracks can form some mighty deep ruts. But that doesn't mean that our thoughts can't be re-routed. At any age we can train our brain to change our mind.

Not long ago, scientists believed our brains stopped growing and changing somewhere early in childhood. After those first few years, scientists believed, we were pretty much stuck with the effects of our early experiences—positive or negative. Now we know that the brain is much more malleable than we had believed. It is capable of positive change throughout our life. This new understanding of the "plasticity" of the brain means that we can retrain ourselves to avoid those deep ruts in our thinking. We can derail that useless thought train.

Here's a quick and easy technique that you can employ anywhere and any time you find yourself under a "thought attack." Let's say you notice your mood has slipped downward. You tune into your thoughts and realize that you've been worrying about an argument you recently had with someone important to you. Like my friend coming out of that "twilight sleep," you realize that while you were driving, or shaving, or standing in line—your mind was replaying the conversation and mentally continuing the argument. As you become aware of those negative, repetitive thoughts—stop. Take a breath. Then remind yourself that a bunch of thoughts are on the "spin cycle" of your mental washing machine.

Sometimes, just that awareness is enough to stop the cycle—or at least to stop being bothered by it. But other times, the impact of the thinking may already be felt throughout your body. Cortisol, the stress hormone, may be pumping through your blood and creating the uncomfortable physical sensations that usually trigger the fight or flight response.

You feel stuck in the hole your mind has dug. At this point, you might want to try envisioning a stop sign and mentally yelling, "Stop" to the incessant thoughts (hear yourself yell "stop" in your own mind, but try to recognize that others don't really need to hear it—so just do it mentally). This may give you some leverage by creating greater distance, objectivity, and neutrality concerning the content of your thoughts.

If this doesn't free you from the storm, then find a distraction to break free of the thought habit. Go out for a run or a swim. Listen to your favorite upbeat playlist. Take a cold shower. Open up a good book—or do whatever strategy helps you to change channels on your mind. Then resolve to stay awake and aware so that you catch a thought sooner and sooner in the process of forming— just by noticing subtle shifts in how you feel.

To break free of that thought rut may or may not require repeated efforts. And you may not end the thought storm as quickly as you'd like. But keep it up. Over time, you'll re-route your automatic responses to better responses. It's a matter of changing your thought habits.

Practicing Good Mental Hygiene

In the early part of the 20th century, the Mental Hygiene Movement reminded people to keep an eye on the thoughts that were running through their heads. It also promoted a heightened awareness of what it is we are "feeding" our minds.

Today, most of what is offered as entertainment actually qualifies as "junk food-for-thought." And as the adage goes, we are what we eat: "garbage in—garbage out." So practicing good mental hygiene involves limiting our exposure to garbage and cultivating an appetite for nutritious food-for-thought that helps us grow stronger as ethical beings. But it is also about choosing the way we allow the "garbage" to hang around in our heads. Do we let those thoughts sit around messing up our mental well-being?

The idea that our thoughts define us is a common misconception. We have thoughts and feelings but they are not who we are. We are meant to be the leader of our mind and to use our thoughts and feelings to motivate and navigate through the world in support of our greater expression. Our mind is our essential tool for doing this, but it was never meant to be in charge. And no doubt you've heard it said, "The mind is a wonderful servant but a terrible master."

People who are thrivers don't stop having thoughts. They just recognize that every thought they have is only that—it's just a thought. And each of us has a choice whether we're going to follow the thought down the rabbit hole or just blow it off and let it go if it has no value.

There is plenty of advice out there on what to do with thoughts. Some believe you should just carry on, acting as if nothing is going on. Hide those negative thoughts. Deny they are there. Unfortunately, they still tend to leak out. Others believe in the "power of positive thinking." Problem is, that requires you to drum up new and better thoughts to take their place. While they may be more positive than the alternative, they are still just thoughts. And it usually becomes tiresome to create a new thought, only to have a negative thought about that new positive thought, requiring yet another positive thought. The other option is just to recognize that a thought is just a thought. It is nothing more or less than that.

In the midst of a cyclone of thinking, if you will remind yourself to step back and watch how quickly negative thoughts can generate uncomfortable feelings—when we let them go on unchecked—you will find those thoughts lose steam, and the negative feelings tend to evaporate. From there you can choose your next steps on your path to gaining greater internal cooperation so you can thrive in your life ever more fully—no matter what.

TL;DR—A Thought Is A Thought

- Our mind is an amazing thing. It has a primary task: create thoughts. Good thoughts, bad thoughts; helpful thoughts, not-so-helpful thoughts; creative thoughts, mundane thoughts—the mind is simply busy, creating thoughts.

- The fact that our mind creates thoughts is not a problem. The fact that we confuse our thoughts with reality *is* a problem. It is easy for us to forget that we are thinking something, and assume that what we are thinking is reality.

- The chances of confusing a thought with reality go up the lower our energy level is. When we are functioning in a low mood, with low energy, we are more likely to confuse a thought with reality.

- Our thoughts are what create our feelings, our emotional life. When we are angry, we can track back and discover that we are thinking about something that is making us angry. And when we confuse the thought with reality, we see our anger as justified and based in reality (instead of being based in a thought).

- We are naturally designed to return to a thriving state, but only when we don't misuse our mind. When we hold onto unhelpful thoughts, we tend to create a "thought storm" that keeps us locked into a painful emotional state. Until we let the thought pass, the emotional state remains. And as soon as we let the thought go, the emotional state begins to dissipate.

- Since we are so used to attaching to the thoughts, holding onto the thoughts, we tend to not notice just how noisy our minds are. It becomes background noise that dominates our emotional lives and colors our reality.

- At any time, if you can use your emotions to track back to the thought. When you are caught in an emotion you would rather not have, focus on the thought that is creating that emotion. Are you thinking about something that is making you angry? Are you focused on a thought that is leaving you feeling hopeless or frustrated? Note the thought, remind yourself that it is only a thought, and release the thought.

- It can take practice to break the mental habits, learned over a lifetime. But the more you practice releasing the thought, the easier it becomes. The easier it becomes, the quicker you return to a better emotional state and state of mind.

Chapter 3

accept what is

"When you argue with reality, you lose—but only 100% of the time."
—Byron Katie

most of us spend a lot of time and energy struggling against *What Is*. One way we do this is by playing what I call the "Life's not fair" game, in which we tell ourselves that somehow we didn't get a fair shake, we didn't get a good start, we didn't get the resources lots of other people got and that should have been coming our way.

Like the lyrics of more than a few country-western songs, we are convinced that "life has done us wrong." It's cheated on us—while giving a fair shake to "that guy over there" who is far less deserving than we are.

We play this sad refrain over and over again in our brain, suffering a little more every time we do, digging ourselves into a deeper hole as we go. Or else, we take solace in the bitter sweetness of our undeserved martyrdom.

As both a chaplain and a coach, I've heard this nearly irresistible refrain sung many times by many people. I must admit, I've sung it a few times myself along the way. But Thrivers know better than to get stuck wasting their time and energy on something so pointless and debilitating as arguing with reality.

Thrivers know that life is challenging enough without compounding our problems with the misery that comes from struggling with what is. As Byron Katie said in the quote at the start of this chapter, when we do, we lose—"but only 100% of the time."

The belief that "This shouldn't be happening to me," or "It never should never have happened this way"—comes from the belief that life has a correct and proper course to follow. When things go "as they should," we believe that our hopes and dreams, plans and actions will all work out to produce the desired results.

If only it was as simple and linear as that! We'd just do the "right" *cause* and then get the desired *effect*. But in this infinitely vast and complex Universe, life unfolds in completely unexpected ways. Is it even valid to try to judge what is "fair" or "unfair?"

Often, the seeming "unfairness of life" is actually weighted in our favor. Life is pretty fragile, so even being alive is unfair. And if you are reading this book, you are in the "unfairly in your favor" category of the population that is literate and has the means to obtain it. I've noticed how many people who told me how unfair life is, seemed to have missed the great fortune of where they were born, how they were raised, and the opportunities provided to them.

The only constant we can count on is change. And the only thing we can accurately predict about Life—other than death and gravity—is that Life is wholly unpredictable. It frequently sends us "curve balls" out of "left field" that force us to drop our plans and run—sometimes in a whole new direction than we had ever hoped or imagined. One of our most reliable survival skills in this suddenly chaotic environment—that allows us to quickly find our footing and thrive no matter what—is *Acceptance Of W hat Is.*

Wasted Indignation

Instead of simply recognizing that life cannot be contained or controlled, we often feel shocked, hurt and certain that there must be some mistake when things go completely off the rails. The mind seeks someone or something to blame. After all, we tell ourselves, we did what we were supposed to do so it wasn't supposed to happen this way. But sometimes it does anyway.

Believing that there's some rightness or wrongness for how life should progress is a surefire way to feel like we're one of the "good people" to whom "bad things" unexpectedly happen. This is not to say that you or I are not good people (or that we are bad people), as much as to state this: things happen to people. Good things happen and bad things happen to everyone. That's just the nature of life.

Another way we have of making our life more difficult is by comparing it with other people who appear to have more than we do—more opportunities, more health, better families or better luck. But as they say in 12-Step meetings, we're comparing our insides with their outsides—our inner pain with their outer appearance of good fortune. As one person in the movie business told me, "We are comparing their final cut with our edits on the floor."

The compulsion to make these comparisons offers only misery as the reward for our indulgence. It keeps us wishing we were more, or had more, or were somewhere else, or even someone else. But if we're really honest with ourselves, and compare our lot with the vast majority of the world, we can see that we're among the very "lucky few."

Not only isn't Life fair, but it doesn't owe us anything. In fact, if we have a place to live, clothes to wear, and food to eat—we're actually in a tiny minority on this planet. We may have strong ideas about the opportunities that should be coming our way, the health we should be enjoying, the quality of relationships we deserve to be in. These are all common desires and it would be wonderful if they were all fulfilled. But often they are not. And when we fight against what is—or what isn't—this state of resistance increases our suffering and diminishes our ability to respond effectively.

The desire for things to be different leads to our resistance. Resistance to *What Is* bogs us down, slows us up, and stresses us out. Period.

Thrivers know that fighting against reality is futile. By accepting reality—at the same time that they seek ways to improve it—they reduce the "inflammation" around the wound of disappointment. They relax into a place of *acceptance* with what is. And in this more positive frame of mind, they more easily find clarity and healing—even in the face of the devastating and unthinkable. For most Thrivers, this is a learned skill that grows stronger with practice.

Here's one of my favorite parables—you may have read some version of it elsewhere.

A Chinese farmer has a beautiful stallion that jumps the fence and runs off one day. His neighbors hear about it and come over to commiserate with the farmer. "Oh, what a terrible thing," they say, shaking their heads in regret for him. But the farmer simply shrugs his shoulders and says, "Well, you know, who's to say what's good or what's bad?!"

A while later the stallion returns—leading a whole herd of brood mares. The farmers' neighbors are amazed at his extraordinary turn of fortune. "How lucky you are," they tell him. But the farmer still shrugs his shoulders and says, "Who really can say what's good or what's bad?"

Then, his strong, young son, while training one of the mares to take a saddle and rider, is thrown by the horse and breaks his leg when he hits the ground. Now, the farmer's neighbors groan for the anticipated consequence of this awful event. "Oh my," they say, "What are you going to do now? You need him to help you bring in the harvest!" After all, they point out, the farmer is not as young and strong as he once was. But still the farmer persists in saying, "Who really knows what's good or what's bad?"

Then, a battle breaks out along the border and the army comes to recruit every strong young man for the front lines—of a war from which none will return.

This little story sums it up very nicely. In the midst of any problem we really can't say what's good or what's bad in the long term. We only know what we'd prefer or not prefer in the moment. What else we know is that resisting *what is* makes things so much more difficult to tolerate. It also interferes with our ability to find workable solutions.

Thrivers know that Grace under Pressure is a bankable skill that we all can develop. But it takes time and practice. Like it or not, life gives us plenty of opportunities for practice.

Shift Happens!

For many years, people have come to me for coaching asking the question, "Why did this have to happen to me?" Part of what they are asking is, "Was there a way for this not to have happened?" They are looking for a way to rewrite what happened and what now is.

When I was a hospital chaplain, people dealing with the aftermath of major accidents or illness would want me to offer a theological explanation of their predicament—a Big Picture view that could make sense of their suffering. But I came to realize that they were really wrestling with the same unhappy question, "How can this NOT happen?"

Instead of saying, "Okay. This has happened. Now I've got to figure out what to do from here," they were constantly asking, "Why did this happen—and is there a way I can undo what has happened?" So, an enduring truth to learn about life can be summed up like this: We can't change What Is. What has happened—has happened.

I came to realize that the question of "Why did this happen?" was often a desire to figure out how not to have had it happen. It was not a theological inquiry, as much as a wish to have it "un-happen." It is a desire for an alternate reality, devoid of that event.

Simply stated, we are where we are. Whatever chain of events brought us to this place left us with this set of circumstances to deal with. When we fight this fact, we become stuck in pain, anger, and resistance, which is not a position of strength and ingenuity. Acceptance is not about self-defeat. It's about recognizing, "This is where I am. Now, how do I build from here?"

Thomas Leonard, who was considered one of the fathers of Life Coaching, had a term to help people reconcile themselves with what is. He called it the "Present Perfect." He wasn't referring to the grammatical sense of that meaning. And he also wasn't saying that everything is just as you would want it to be.

What Leonard *was* saying was that the present is a perfect amalgamation of everything that has come before it—both seen and unseen. And the sooner and more completely we move into a place of surrendered acceptance to what is, the sooner our mind can conceive a course of corrective actions, moving out from and beyond what is. When we're in acceptance of what is, our energy is also more likely to attract more of what it is we truly desire.

Facing What Is

Many times, I've talked with people who were over their heads in debt. Their bills were mounting; they were paying the minimum amount on their credit cards—yet they could not accept the fact that, financially, they were on the edge of ruin. They were already "upside down" but pretending they could go on like this indefinitely. Yet, all it would take was one glitch with their car or their health and they'd find themselves over the edge.

I encouraged them to spread everything out on the table, and then calculate all the debt and all the income to get an accurate picture of their situation. Once they saw the difference between the two figures, they would finally be in a position to say, "Okay, now where do we go from here? Let's develop a strategy and take appropriate action." Without acceptance, there is no moving forward.

This seems obvious and logical, doesn't it? The problem is that when we're in the midst of any scary situation, we're less likely to approach it logically. We don't really *want* to come face-to-face with the irrefutable facts of our situation. But until we do, we can't improve it.

This applies to our relationships as well as every other aspect of our life. I have coached people who were in denial of the fact that their relationship was falling apart—until one day they could no longer avoid acknowledging the reality. Many times, it was their partner's words, "This is not working for me," that finally penetrated their defenses, forcing them to face the facts. What a scary, painful moment that is. But until we're no longer struggling to avoid the truth, we can't find a starting point for rebuilding our lives.

This applies equally to our careers and every other area of life. Without a realistic assessment and acceptance of what is—no improvement is possible.

Facing Facts is NOT the Same as Accepting Defeat

"When the going gets tough, the tough get going"—but often in the wrong direction. In the face of what may seem overwhelmingly negative odds, the impulse is to run away or just give up. One of the core differences between Thrivers and others is that at some point, Thrivers are able to set aside their "give-up" impulse and decide to go with their "get-up" response so they can move ahead.

This difference in approach highlights the significant distinction between giving up and surrendering to what is. Giving up is declaring defeat and collapsing into a place of despair and despondency. Acceptance involves a clear assessment of our situation, the letting go of our resistance to the inevitable, and the full-on understanding of what is now transpiring. This then enables us to do as Thrivers do, which is to use everything for our learning and growth. Thrivers know that even in a seeming "defeat," the seeds of a future victory can be harvested.

The longer we put off facing the facts and resisting the reality of our situation, the more we delay our ability to take what we can learn from what has happened and use it to propel ourselves forward. The longer we resist it, the more deeply we dig into the current hole. I remember some very painful lessons I learned when I was working on building a business that eventually collapsed completely. I was reluctant to read the early signs that this business was headed for failure. So I kept pumping money into it in hopes that I could save it. But I couldn't—and because of my resistance, I was in greater debt than I would have been.

When I finally said, "I can't keep doing this—I have to make a change," I was flooded with insights and the awareness of how I could do things differently in my next business enterprise. What I saw was the importance of being clear about my core values and financial commitment right from the outset. These were very valuable lessons that made it possible for me to achieve success in my next business. But until I was willing to accept that my business was beyond saving, I was unable to see the potential for growth that was there for me all along.

Many times, over the years, I've spoken with successful people who have had major business failures in the past. My question always was, "Why do you think it failed?" Almost invariably, the ones who are the Thrivers will say something like—"Because I wasn't ready for success back then." Or, "I couldn't face what was really going on there until it was too late." Or, "I needed the lessons that I gained from this failure in order to achieve the success I now have."

Taking Full Responsibility is Fully Empowering

When we refuse to accept what is, we also refuse to accept responsibility for what went wrong and for where we can go from here. We end up where we are, stuck with what has happened, and unable to move forward until we take responsibility.

Whatever the cause of the failure, when we accept responsibility for it, we recognize that we also have the power to do things differently next time. Otherwise, if we insist that we aren't responsible—remembering that responsibility is not the same as fault and blame—then we are powerless to make things better. In order to thrive and to use our setbacks to catapult us toward success, we need to be able to say, "Here's what happened and here's where I am. What must I do in order to get where I want to go?"

Taking responsibility also shifts us out of wishing things were different into planning and acting to improve them. Regret for the past, dwelling on what could have been, bemoaning our fate—only delay the process of moving ahead. They also burden our mind with a greater sense of failure and hopelessness. The thriving person steps up and says, "Here's where I am. I know what needs to happen and now I'm going to move forward."

Part of Acceptance of What Is—is the acceptance that we really don't know what is in our best interests. We only think we know. Here's a famous statement by the 19th century Irish writer, Oscar Wilde that is helpful to keep in mind: "There are only two tragedies in life: One is not getting what one wants, and the other is getting it."

Whether you like her music or not, and whether you agree with her life choices or not, the pop singer Madonna made a very wise observation during an interview. The interviewer asked, "Is there anything you would change, any choices you would do differently?" Madonna, surprising the interviewer, said "No. Everything that has happened in my life has made me who I am. That is why I am here today."

For the most part, we cannot see the bigger patterns of our lives until years later—in retrospect. Thus, we cannot see how the tough times and struggles of today are actually strengthening and preparing us for whatever we may meet down the road. But if we could see the value to be gained from meeting our current challenges head-on, we might well realize that it's a good thing we can't avoid the struggles. For if we could, we would likely lose the opportunity to enlarge our capacity to skillfully deal with whatever lies ahead.

Still, no matter how skillful we may be in turning "lemons into lemonade," we cannot skip the grieving process for our losses in the moment. Only once we have allowed ourselves to mourn our disappointments can we see how they may serve us as gateways into something else of enormous value that could not have come about in any other way.

What we have to do to survive and surmount the pain of the loss can turn out to become the defining moment or strategy for our lives. It may deepen and expand our hearts. It could open up new vistas and avenues of exploration and discovery for us. And likely, it both compelled and enabled us to find ways of being of greater service in the world.

In giving more love, compassion, and support to ourselves and others—since all of us must go through the ups and downs of life's scary, thrilling roller-coaster—we fill our own hearts with healing and pleasure. And when we hold the positive intention to do so, then ultimately all things must work together for good in our life—even if we're not able to see this until later.

🌀 TL;DR—Accept What Is 🌀

- We spend too much energy with what "should be," rather than "what is." We stay trapped in fighting against our current situation and the life events/choices that have gotten us to here. That is a losing battle.
- When people say, "This shouldn't be happening to me," or "Life isn't fair," they are fighting against *what is*, even though it is "What is.
- Many people confuse "acceptance" with giving up. But "accepting what is" creates the starting point of moving to something new. If you can't accept where you are, it is impossible to accurately decide where you are moving toward. Accepting "What Is" establishes the beginning point of your new journey.
- Two big barriers are the games of "What Should Be" and "What I Believe To Be." The "should be" is rooted in the "Life and Fairness" myth. Life isn't designed to be fair. And if you are able to read this book, you are most likely well on the side of the fairness weighted *in* your favor— NOT *against* you. And the "What I Believe To Be" has a fatal flaw when it is based in what is really not. Many times, we believe ourselves to be in a better or worse position than we are, simply because we haven't paused to evaluate and accept.
- "Accepting What Is" becomes the foundation of accepting responsibility (not blame) of choosing what to do and how to do it.

Chapter 4

forgive quickly
and move forward

When stories of radical forgiveness appear in the news, they move us all deeply. A mother forgives and educates her child's killer when he comes out of prison. A man left bereft by the murder of his son joins forces with the father of the boy who committed the murder to spread the word of reconciliation and forgiveness at events around the country. By so doing, they heal their own hearts.

Thrivers strive to forgive as quickly as possible because they understand something about forgiveness that is easily forgotten in the midst of our pain and anger over something "completely unforgivable:" We forgive for ourselves. When we forgive another person, we release our hearts from the chronic inner torment of hurt and resentment that have been weighing us down since the incident occurred.

I knew a minister years ago who grew up in the projects of an inner city somewhere in the U.S. When he was 12 years old, walking home from school, he and his best friend were attacked by a group of older boys. His friend was stabbed to death by two of their assailants.

The shock, pain, and trauma left the future minister speechless for months after. After years of struggling with this painful and traumatic event, he was finally able to forgive and let go of the outrage and bitterness that had festered in his core since that time so long before. And with the letting go came the realization that this horrendous act, which took his best friend from him, had actually initiated him onto his life purpose—a path of service to others that has brought him such fulfillment.

As a minister, this man practices and preaches the power of forgiveness, which all of us desire to experience for all the ways we so frequently fall short of our own and other's expectations. He speaks with an authenticity and persuasion that only someone who has lived through such a transformative experience can possibly express.

What this man knows and teaches with such power and eloquence is that when we choose to extend forgiveness to another person, we are actually freeing ourselves from the prison of our own resentment. In no way does forgiveness mean that we are condoning or dismissing what has happened. The letting go, the forgiving is a release for one's self. It is not releasing the other from their actions, but releasing ourselves from their actions.

Why should we want to do that? Because relationships that don't end well don't end. We remain energetically tethered by the power of our strong emotional connections to the very person who has caused us so much grief—until we find forgiveness in our heart and let them go.

The Ritual of Forgiveness

When I was growing up, my brother and I were constantly tussling. Only 18 months apart, we were a couple of unruly bear cubs, my mother would often say.

Sometimes, in the midst of an altercation, my father would wade in between us, take us both by the scruff of the neck, and insist that we apologize to each other. Not only that, but we were also to say, "I forgive you." Under duress, we certainly did as we were told. But the words we spoke were far from true. The fight was over—but only for the moment.

Forgiving under pressure as a ritual of reconciliation has little power to release the toxic thoughts and feelings we may hold against another. In fact, it may even heighten our resentment and foster resistance to creating a new beginning in a relationship.

But that is how we have been taught forgiveness. It is done under pressure, for the other person, but without a real internal shift. We *know* we should. So, we might mouth words of forgiveness. But we continue to harbor the toxic thoughts in our heart.

In truth, forgiveness never really happens when it's handled as an obligation. True forgiveness is something we can choose to give to someone else as part of our own process of healing the misery that our own animosity creates in us. In close relationships, when both parties forgive and take responsibility for the rift their discord has created, their bond of affection and intimate connection is actually strengthened and deepened.

At the very least, it allows the forgiver the opportunity to move forward, unencumbered by the hurt and pain of the past -- or, more accurately, the story one tells oneself about the past. Since we rarely remember things as they occurred, we often gloss over our own place of responsibility and participation.

Why It Can Be So Hard to Forgive

Forgiveness is a loaded word and greatly misunderstood in this culture. When I say that thrivers know how to forgive, some people will say, "Well, you shouldn't have to do that because forgiveness is something that somebody must earn."

That's why I want to redefine what forgiveness actually is—and what it can do for us. As I see it, forgiveness is about *choosing* to let go of the *impact* of an event. It's offering yourself the opportunity to regain the energy that's wasted when you hold onto the hurts, the slights, and the pains of the past.

It is not about pretending something didn't happen. It is not pretending there was no pain. It is not pretending that sometimes, people actually mean to do something cruel and violent (although many times, even purposeful hurt comes from that person's place of hurt). It is about letting go of the impact on us.

I'm aware that when I don't want to forgive, I'm spending a lot of energy holding onto something I didn't like in the first place. And, I like it even less the longer I let it live in my heart and mind. When I choose to forgive, I free my heart and walk away from the residue of toxic emotions and recycled memories of a very painful situation.

As part of the forgiveness process, we also attend to our pain and anger and grieve the losses we have suffered. And we need to understand that forgiving is not about letting someone else "off the hook." Our forgiveness does not condone or exonerate someone's actions. Nor does it leave us on the losing end of an unhappy relationship. What it does is cut the energetic umbilical cord that binds us to the person who engendered so much pain in us.

A secondary reason why forgiveness can be so difficult may relate to our survival instinct. We are designed to scan the environment and be on the alert for threats. If someone has hurt us in the past, we may—rightly or wrongly—equate that person with danger. Our evolutionary wiring leads us to hold onto every hurt, every slight, every pain we've experienced as a result of an interaction with another person as a strategy for self-protection. But what it does, instead, is keep us in the wary victim mode, rather than enabling us to move through life from a place of empowerment, discernment, and inner freedom.

Staying Stuck

Unforgiveness exacts a toll on us. It can keep us mired in hurt and anger, which preoccupies our mind and saps our strength. Just notice what happens in your body when you're nursing a grievance. Your breath gets shallow, your body gets tense, and your blood pressure may rise.

Your mind keeps churning on what happened. You re-live the event in your thoughts, and your body follows right along. It acts as if you are going through the event right then. And we humans tend to repeat that process over and over.

When hurt and anger are allowed to simmer without being effectively processed and released, they can turn into toxic resentment, which is harmful to body and mind. Forgiveness offers us the opportunity to release the resentment and end the toxicity. When we begrudge our forgiveness, we deprive ourselves of that relief. We also maintain our status as "victim" in the story of what happened to us.

That very story is the theme of so many songs: We've been wronged, we can't let it go, and we hold the other person responsible forever for their betrayal. Part of the problem with that scenario is that it acts as an unconscious deterrent to thriving. While success may be the best revenge for some, others hold onto their wounds as a constant indictment of the person who inflicted them. In this scenario, they are absolved of responsibility for their own life and well-being. As the victim, the burden for "making things right" is with the perpetrator. The perpetrator may be unwilling or even unaware. Thus, the victim remains stuck waiting for the other person to make amends—to take it back or make it better. What a way to stunt one's own growth.

Myths About Forgiveness

For some, the phrase, "Forgive and Forget" may act as a deterrent to forgiving because it's virtually impossible to simply forget a wrong that has been done to us. So, if we believe that forgiving requires forgetting, then it will be forever beyond us.

We may never forget what happened to us. But we can release ourselves from the tight grip unforgiveness holds on our heart. With time, we may even develop an understanding of the reasons behind another person's actions and have compassion for them.

A woman I know who suffered a lifetime of pain at the hands of her parents was eventually able to see how instrumental that experience was to the development of her extraordinary body of creative work. Her pain also led her to pursue healing and self-development to a level beyond what most people achieve in a lifetime. Having received so little love or validation from her parents, she has a profound understanding of how important they are, so she offers warmth and validation to people everywhere she goes. She also recognizes that it was because her parents never received what they needed from their parents that they were never able to give it to their children. They didn't even know it was missing.

One of the keys to forgiveness that she found so helpful comes from *The Four Agreements* by Don Miguel Ruiz. (Agreement #2)

a) "Don't take anything personally. Nothing others do is because of you.
b) What others say and do is a projection of their own reality, their own dream.
c) When you are immune to the opinions and actions of others, you won't be the victim of needless suffering."

I would add a fourth point to the 2nd Agreement, a key belief of mine—which is to remember that *everyone is doing the best they can, given where they are.* This does not mean that people always give an "optimal performance," or that we all are the best we *can* be. It's that people do the best they can, given their current circumstances, past conditioning, and life condition in the moment.

Another myth about forgiveness is that it is the same as reconciliation. In reality, these are two very different, often unrelated processes. You can forgive somebody but have nothing further to do with them. Or, you can forgive somebody and decide how you're going to enter back into a relationship with them and what the terms of the relationship will be going forward.

Forgiveness is about letting go. Reconciliation is about reconnecting with the other person. Forgiveness is an intrapersonal process. It takes place inside our self and has nothing to do with the other person. Reconnecting and reconciliation are interpersonal. They can only occur in relationship to the other person. The difference here is profound.

When we forgive, we let go of the pain of what happened and reclaim the energy required to hold a grudge. We recognize that forgiveness is a kindness we do for ourselves as part of our process of healing from our suffering. With this understanding, we suddenly see that everything is forgivable, if we choose to take that on. No matter how heinous an act, we can always come to a place of forgiveness in our heart that releases **us** from the iron fist of hurt and rage.

This leads us to another myth about forgiveness that has been a big stumbling block for many people. It is the idea that forgiveness is a weakness—that it's about giving in, knuckling under, and letting the other person off the hook. But nothing could be further from the truth. In the words of Mahatma Gandhi, "The weak can never forgive. Forgiveness is the attribute of the strong."

When people choose to forgive, they're taking back their strength, they're taking back their power, and they're giving up that stuck place of victimhood that has held them hostage for so long. Forgiveness is a profoundly courageous act.

Forgiveness is a Process

Forgiveness is simple but not easy. The biggest challenge is that we must overcome our own blocks and retrain our mind toward a perpetual attitude of forgiveness. This can happen by following a series of steps. The more we practice the steps required to do this, the easier it becomes and the more rapidly we can let go of the cumulative pain that so many of us drag through life.

The first step in the process is to see the other person's humanness, rather than dehumanizing them as the enemy. When we recognize that all humans are imperfect—that we do the best we can in any given moment but are flawed, error-prone creatures that sometimes create enormous suffering and damage for others—then we can more readily connect with the empathy in our hearts.

As we build empathy, we gain an inside understanding of the other person's motivations and suffering. We move away from stereotypes and assumptions and avoid what in psychology is known as the "attribution error," which looks something like this: If I do something wrong, I see that I've made a mistake. But if *you* do something wrong, I'm more likely to see it as stemming from something inherently wrong with you.

In the attribution error, I let myself off the hook while indicting you as possessing a permanent character defect. It's a whole lot harder to forgive someone I perceive as having some inherent personality flaw—which then keeps me locked in unforgiveness and a false sense of superiority.

Here's another way of seeing things that may be useful. It's a statement attributed to various people. But whoever first spoke these words offered us all a very liberating perspective: "If we could read the secret history of our enemies, we should find in each man's life sorrow and suffering enough to disarm all hostility."

Once we recognize that the person who did us harm is another struggling, error-prone human being, then we can take the **second step** in the process of forgiveness. It is the actual decision to travel the path toward total forgiveness. No action is required with this step—only the decision and commitment to see it through. This is the step in which we take back our power.

Have you heard it said that, "resentment is like swallowing poison and then waiting for the other person to die"? The only person who suffers the injury of our resentment and lack of forgiveness is the person who refuses to forgive.

In this simple (not easy) step, one makes a firm commitment to move toward forgiveness and to stop swallowing the poison of resentment. This is not about arriving at forgiveness, but about choosing to move toward forgiveness. It is a decision to move ahead, not an indication of completion of the process.

Step number three is to breathe through the emotions and hurts. Don't try to push the feelings away, to analyze or process them. In this moment, just let yourself experience them as you breathe deeply. Be present with yourself as you would with a hurt and grieving child. Once they are acknowledged and allowed, the painful feelings will begin to let go of their grip on you—for now. They may return again some other time. But with this strategy you will be able to continually drain the reservoir of built-up pain. And each time you release a little more, a little more sunshine comes into your heart.

The type of breathing that will be the most helpful to you through this process is the kind employed in yoga, meditation, singing, or playing a wind instrument. It's the deep, relaxed belly breathing that we do so naturally as children but forget to do when we're older and we're under stress and tension.

It's how we're naturally built to breathe. But the more accustomed we get to the stress and pressure of living, the more habituated we become to shallow chest breathing. So, here's how to re-learn belly breathing: Lie on your back with one hand over your belly button and the other on your chest bone. As you inhale, the hand on your belly should move out. Your hand on your chest bone should remain still. As you exhale, the hand on your belly moves back down. Do this for a few minutes, so you can get the body memory of breathing in that way. Then you can belly breathe as you're sitting up and standing up. Let it become a habit. At least let it become a conscious choice when you are feeling those painful emotions.

Part of what happens in pressured situations when fear and upset are running through us—which is what happens when we're gripped by hurt, rage, and unforgiveness—is that we get caught in "fight-or-flight mode." But we can override our brain's natural tendency to go there by going back to the deep belly breathing. This is a conscious method of breathing that moves us back to calm.

When a traumatic memory replays an event in which you felt so grievously injured, you can breathe through it with the awareness that our mind is actually designed to let those things go, to move through the emotional responses and negative thoughts, and return to a normal state.

When we hold onto the upset, we actually go against our own mind's natural healing process. We also give greater power to what is first just a thought—the memory of a painful event from the past. By so doing, we bring the hurt and anger back to life. Instead, we can choose just to allow the thought to move through us simply by witnessing it and breathing through it without ever engaging it.

As we breathe through our belly, the energy of the memory is allowed to process, pass through us, and leave our body. We are not hanging on to it and giving it more life through our renewed attention. And as it diminishes in intensity, it allows us to return to a normal state. As we do that, we begin to allow the healing to occur that happens in our psyche when we're not suppressing our thoughts and feelings or trying to analyze them down to the smallest little details.

Now, I know this is easier said than done. I have a client who went through a highly abusive and traumatic childhood but has since worked toward forgiveness. He still finds that he is susceptible to getting triggered into the "old stuff."

He equates this periodic return of toxic memories with the recurrence of malaria some sufferers experience. In the past, he would be laid low by it because the waves of negative stories and feelings would overcome him. Like a magnet, they would gather up all similar kinds of experiences throughout his life—in which his childhood drama played out in his adult relationships—and the pain would be too much for him.

Now, however, he treats himself with great care and kindness when the toxic memories and his own reactivity move through him. Thus, the process takes a much shorter time and never knocks him out of commission. It also occurs ever more infrequently.

The fourth step in the forgiveness process is extremely valuable to our inner growth. It is the dawning recognition, acceptance—and for some people, great appreciation—of the gifts and lessons the incident, and ensuing healing process, precipitated in them.

Finding the lessons and gifts from the painful events in our past takes time as well as willingness. But these gifts are very present and profound for those who have worked their way through the process of forgiving and letting go. I deeply appreciate how such people are described in this beautiful quote from Dr. Elizabeth Kubler-Ross:

> "The most beautiful people we have known are those who have known defeat, known suffering, known struggle, known loss, and have found their way out of the depths. These persons have an appreciation, a sensitivity, and an understanding of life that fills them with compassion, gentleness, and a deep loving concern. Beautiful people do not just happen."

Discovering the gift and the learning that comes packaged in a trauma allows us to gain value from the experience while letting the hurt fade away. Sometimes, what you learn has to do with the need for greater discernment in the company you keep, or greater boundaries in your relationships. The decisions that you make, the places that you go, the situations that you put yourself into—may all be up for review and re-evaluation.

Sometimes, the lesson is a self-realization that you are tougher than you may have guessed. You may discover a tenacity that you hadn't noticed before, as the struggle called forth new efforts on your part.

Other times, the lesson and gift may be empathy for people in similar situations and struggles. It is not a simple "sympathy," but a deep empathy, since you have already trodden that path.

As we sort through the broken shards to find the diamonds that were formed by the pressure we were under, we may move into a place within our own heart where peace, gratitude and forgiveness are ever-present. And this is the gift that we give to ourselves when we give up our identity as a victim. Now we are in the flow of the process of restoring ourselves and regaining our personal power. Then, whatever happens next, we have a way to move through it again and gain from it—like scaling one mountain peak and then another.

This stage is not about making everything rosy and happy. Tough things happen in every life. Life is "full contact." There are painful and tough times. And in every painful or tough time, there is an opportunity for self-discovery and learning. There are new layers of self-awareness, mental toughness, and resilience that can emerge in response to the challenge. And sometimes, there is the revealing of a new path for a renewed life.

One important note is necessary here: learning lessons and distilling skills from a painful incident is not the same as believing that the event was put upon you to teach you a lesson. It is the recognition that there are always invaluable gifts, skills, and learnings that can be gleaned from tough life struggles.

The fifth step in the process is particularly tricky, because it requires us to take responsibility for what has happened to us. This is not about blaming the victim. It's about discovering whether we played some role in precipitating the event *and/or* in holding on to the pain that it caused in us. Perhaps someone's actions devastated life as we knew it and we've been stuck waiting for this person to make amends all these years before moving on.

Sometimes you can look back and say, "Wow. I created an association with somebody that I knew in my heart wasn't safe." Or, "I put myself in a situation that I sensed from the beginning was highly risky."

Taking radical responsibility like this can be a chastening experience but it's also an enlightening one. When we look to see where we might have been complicit in creating great pain for ourselves, we now have the roadmap for bypassing such experiences in the future. And if we ask inwardly, "What was my pay-off for going along with this for so long?" we may never again be willing to compromise our happiness for such counterfeit compensation.

Wash, Rinse, Repeat

The sixth and final step in the process of forgiveness is the realization that forgiveness is a process—it's not an event. It's not something that happens once and for all and then we're back to normal, though perhaps "sadder but wiser."

Forgiveness is a way of being and moving through the world—because hurts will continue to occur throughout our life. And issues that may once have seemed resolved can recur or be re-stimulated. Then we find ourselves having to redo the forgiveness process and reinforce our willingness to let go of the hurt and pain, learn from the experience, and move on in our life.

Again, this is easier said than done. When we can get triggered back into fight-or-flight reactivity, it may feel safer to hold on to the old familiar pain than to risk the freedom that comes from letting it go. People coming out of prison after years behind bars don't automatically know how to enjoy and make use of the freedom that comes from taking responsibility for themselves.

When we hit another speed bump on the journey of our life, suddenly up come the memories of what occurred the last time that happened. Then, we have to reprocess them again, to breathe through the thoughts and feelings, and then let them go once more.

Healing is not a linear process in which we go through the six steps and we're home free. There is no clean path out. Only a path through. By focusing on getting to forgiveness, you venture through the steps, find yourself on an old step, and work toward a forgiving heart again. The process, though, is based on a decision to get to forgiveness, regardless of the path.

Forgiving For Yourself

How do you reinforce the decision to forgive? You accept the fact that forgiveness is the path to take to liberate yourself from the pain of your past. As long as we hold onto the myth that not forgiving is protection, then we're frozen in place.

When we can accept that the way forward is forgiveness, the way to restore ourselves is forgiveness, the way to find a new path in the world is forgiveness— then we are eager to do whatever it takes to reach that authentic place of forgiveness in our hearts. Our forgiveness does not require the presence of the other person. But when we get to the point where we would be willing to extend our forgiveness face-to-face with that person, then we find ourselves even freer to move forward without being encumbered by the hurts and pains of the past. We can move freely in a new direction and make connections with other people who are also further along in their process of healing and awakening.

Again, forgiveness is not about forgetting. Forgiveness is not about letting the other person off the hook. Forgiveness is not even *for* the other person. It's primarily *for* you. It's accepting that people make mistakes. It's accepting that people do bad things and accepting that you do not have to be a prisoner to what has happened to you. You don't have to be prisoner to the hurts and pains of the past.

You simply have to decide to let them go, learn the lessons they bring to your door, and move forward with a heightened understanding of who you are and what you desire to be in the world. As you do so, you master one of the key skills for thriving, which is to forgive quickly and ever-more fully, to learn from the experience, and to move ahead in the direction of your dreams.

Forgiveness Makes Way for Grace

Remember that minister I mentioned at the beginning of this chapter—whose best friend was brutally attacked and killed by bullies when they were 12 years old? By some strange twist of Fate, Chance, Providence—or whatever you want to call it—the minister found himself face-to-face with the two people who had so dramatically, recklessly and permanently altered his life. The encounters took place at two different times and places.

One day, when the minister was on a plane flying across the country, he walked past a man who was sitting and reading the Bible. He inquired about his interest and his occupation and learned that the man did philanthropic work in South America.

They began conversing together and discovered that they came from the same city. As they inquired further, they learned that they even came from the same neighborhood. As they started sharing the stories of their lives in the neighborhood, the minister described the murder of his friend. The man on the plane was shocked and saddened. He confessed to the minister that he was one of the assailants.

So what had become of his life since that brutal, defining moment? He shared that he'd been so gripped with guilt and remorse since then that the only way he could expiate the pain was to dedicate himself to a life of total service. Now, at last, he had the opportunity to apologize from the depths of his heart to his new friend on the plane. And the minister had the pleasure of accepting the apology and extending his whole-hearted forgiveness.

TL;DR—Forgive Quickly and Move Forward

- The ability to forgive is a hallmark of people who thrive. They are not captured by the sleights, both perceived and real, that come along in living with other people, in a world where things happen.
- We often carry misunderstandings about forgiveness.
  - Forgiveness is NOT about "letting someone off the hook." It is about freeing yourself from that stuck place. Forgiving is primarily for the forgiver, not the forgiven.
  - Forgiveness is NOT about "forgive and forget." We can't simply forget the events in our life that have caused pain. But we can view them differently, and understand the roles in those events differently.
  - Forgiveness is NOT a "have to," but a "choose to" and a "get to," so that the forgiver has the opportunity to move forward, unencumbered by the hurt.
  - Forgiveness is NOT the same as reconciliation. Forgiving is one process. Deciding whether to reestablish the relationship is an entirely separate process. Someone can choose to forgive, but still have a healthy separation from the other person, as a way of preserving safe boundaries.
- Our brains are wired to look for threats and remember the hurts, in an attempt to avoid the hurt in the future. This brain is less designed for the current social fabric as the more dangerous times when encounters could be dangerous or deadly. Yet, we still respond as if they are—even when it is simply the angry voice or actions of a boss, neighbor, friend, or spouse.
- There is a process to forgiving:
  1. See the other person's humanness, building empathy and acceptance that people do the best they can, where they are.
  2. Make the decision to forgive. Simply a choice to move in that direction.

3. Breathe (belly breathing) through the emotions and hurts, as they arise. Acknowledge and allow the pain to move through you, and out.

4. Look for the lessons and gifts of the hurts. Bad things don't happen to you to teach you a lesson. But you may still find lessons there. And gifts we all have come through the struggles we have, if we allow them to emerge.

5. Take responsibility for where you are, where you have been, and where you are headed. This is not about blame, but responsibility.

6. Repeat the process as necessary. Forgiveness is a process, not an event. As new things emerge, repeat the process.

- Remember that part of the forgiveness process is forgiving yourself. You can offer yourself the same empathy and understanding you offer others. Remember that, just like everyone else, YOU are doing the best you can, where you are.

Chapter 5

assume 100% responsibility

taking 100% responsibility for our lives is the key to freedom. That may sound ironic, especially since we so often confuse taking responsibility with taking the blame. Responsibility is NOT the same as blame. But paradoxically, when we do take full responsibility, we end up feeling a whole lot lighter and freer than we do when we avoid it.

The reason this is so may be because when we take full responsibility, we're operating from an empowered place in which we experience ourselves as larger than our challenges and issues. So, here's something that Thrivers have learned: What may seem harder to do at first often ends up being a whole lot easier than the "easy way out," which can turn out to be the long-way around.

Let me give you an example from my own life. Some years ago, when I was at the beginning of my career, I found myself working in the poorest neighborhood in the city. I remember staring out the window of my hot, cramped office wondering, "What am I doing here?!" The teenagers I was counseling came in to see me not because they thought I could help them but because they were ordered to do so by the court. That's not an easy group to work with, as you can well imagine.

Before I came to this office, I was working at a counseling center in a nicer part of town. We were located in an affluent neighborhood that didn't have enough clients to keep this particular counseling program busy. Teens in that area who got into trouble with the law were usually sent home to their families instead of being put through the court system. So, I was loaned out to this cross-town office to do what I could with the frequently resentful youth who were sent there by the courts—often simply due to where they lived, not because of the offense.

That particular day, I was staring out the window, feeling sorry for myself. Another wrestling match of a session with another client reminded me that I was running, yet again, headfirst into a wall of resistance. I was tired, disheartened, and ready to give up. I realized that I had three options: I could sit there feeling miserable indefinitely and collect my paycheck at the end of each pay period. Or, I could get up and go, return to the other office—leaving it all behind.

OR, there was the third option: I could find a way to transform the entire program and work to become more effective with our particular clientele. This option was definitely the most challenging but also the most exciting. I felt a shift in my gut when I considered it.

It was clear to me that these kids really needed the support of people who cared. And they needed some effective solutions to their dead-end lives if they were ever going to turn things around for themselves. So, I started to feel really motivated. What had seemed a few minutes before like a prison sentence now looked like a priceless opportunity to do something that had meaning to me and value to all who would be served if I succeeded in my newfound purpose.

The idea of finding a new approach really energized me. I started to get pro-active. I began writing grant proposals, making requests, and talking with the other counselors about what we needed and what we could accomplish together at this inner city counseling center.

I realized that the only way for us to get from where we were to where I saw that we could be was if I took full responsibility for the shifts I knew we had to make. Someone had to "run with the ball" and I decided that someone would be me. That single realization and determination was the key to my liberation and to the transformation of the entire program into one that truly served the community.

Becoming Fully Responsible

For many of us, the idea of taking full responsibility sounds both daunting and unpleasant. We remember those moments when a parent or teacher pointed to a mess and said in an angry, accusative voice: "Who's responsible for this?" And if we were the "culprit," our heart sank because we knew that we were in trouble. So "taking responsibility" can seem like another way of saying "taking the blame" and being judged "wrong," "bad," or "not okay."

However, if you look up the word in the dictionary, you'll find that **responsibility** also carries other, more empowering meanings. The responsible person is the one in control who manages people and things. To be responsible also means to have the ability to think and act rationally and in a mature fashion.

These meanings are attractive to most all adults. They're also what small children are inspired to emulate when they play "grown-up" with each other. All of us want to believe we're rational and mature. And we want to be the one "in charge" of whatever it is we're doing. However, the fear of failing—and of being blamed and judged for a lack of success—deters many people from stepping up and taking responsibility.

But Wait! There's another meaning to Responsibility that may offer a solution to this dilemma. It's not in the dictionary but it has gained a lot of recent popularity. And it comes directly from the word itself: *Responsibility* can be seen as meaning having the *Ability to Respond* rather than to react automatically or instinctually. We are Response-Able.

That Tiny Gap

Thrivers recognize that we all have the *ability* to respond rather than react—100% of the time. However, it takes conscious and diligent intention and on-going practice to become aware of the tiny gap that exists between a triggering event and our habitual, reflexive reactions to it. Yet within that gap resides a fleeting opportunity to act responsibly and thereby to create a new and more positive outcome for ourselves and everyone else.

The psychiatrist and Holocaust survival Dr. Viktor Frankl—who observed people living under the most extreme conditions in a Nazi concentration camp—observed that, "Between stimulus and response, there is a space. In that space is our power to choose our response. In our response lies our growth and our freedom."

It's in that split-second that we can shift our thinking from—"Well, that's not my problem, that's not my fault, there's nothing I can do about it," to "I'm going to assume there *is* something I *can* do differently and I'm going to take that challenge on."

When we make that shift, we discover that we don't have to be run like a robot by our automatic reactions. We really can do things more responsibly. And the more we choose to do so, the more quickly our old patterns lose their power over us and fade away.

Yes, it does feel more "natural" just to react as we usually do—except that then we get pulled into a repetition of bad situations and end up making it worse. When, instead, we hold the intention to stay conscious and rational in our response, we have the capacity to either change the outcome or deal with it from a more neutral place.

Jack Canfield frames this interaction as a mathematical equation: E + R = O. This stands for Event + Response = Outcome. He points out that an outcome is not just the result of some event happening to us. It starts with the Event, but then we have to factor in how we choose to Respond to the event. That response can have an enormous impact on the Outcome.

Canfield points out that many times, we wander through life assuming that the events (over which we have no control) are the same as the outcome. He notes (echoing Frankl) that we only need to attend to our response—our choice of dealing with the events. It is the combination of the two (Event and Response) that creates the outcome.

Sometimes, how we respond makes all the difference in the world on how events unfold. Other times, the only difference it makes is on how we feel and fare as we experience the outcome. We do not have full control over the Outcome. We simply have more control than if we forget the R of the equation.

Either way, exercising our Ability to Respond is a no-fail approach. We may not succeed in getting exactly what we want, because there are some things over which we have no control. But we will have improved our selves in the process. We will have endeavored to do our very best. We will have pursued a noble goal by taking responsibility for everything within our control. And by so doing, we will have created a different outcome within ourselves—regardless of what happens around us.

No Fault Responsibility

Blame is what we do when we give the lion's share of responsibility for creating and/or fixing a problem to the other person. A therapist I know joked that when a married couple comes in to see him, they race to claim the "victim's chair," as if the other person was the sole cause of all their difficulties.

Of course, we know it's rarely as cut-and-dry as that. But it can certainly feel one-sided to both people in a relationship—with each one certain that they are the injured party and that the problems in the relationship are the other person's fault. Each person plays the game of "finger pointing," simply by choosing where the story begins—choosing the point in the event that makes them appear to be the victim.

There is also an energetic interaction that occurs between people and precipitates their unconscious reactive behaviors. That's why people who desire to thrive endeavor to become more aware and responsible for themselves on all levels—especially when it comes to attracting trouble.

For instance, a woman who was beaten by her father may be drawn to a man who grew up believing that husband's just "naturally" abuse their wives. Even so, if the injured spouse gives away all the responsibility to the offending party/parties, he is also giving away all of the power to make constructive changes.

That's why it's so important—no matter what happens and no matter who did what to whom—that we preserve our right to respond to a situation in a more rational, strategic and empowered way. This is a muscle we can develop—as

I'll explain shortly. But first we have to take responsibility for our lives regardless of what's showing up in the moment.

If The Building Is On Fire. . .

Many times, when I bring up the question of responsibility, people naturally slide back into the "blame game." "So," they often say, "you are saying that everything that happens to me is my fault."

Funny how easy it is for us to drop back into those old beliefs about fault, blame, and responsibility. They are not the same thing. *In fact, the blame game ends up being just a long journey to find the enemy, not the solution.*

To be clear, things happen. Bad weather can strike us at any time. Illness can beset us at any point, regardless of how well or poorly we have taken care of ourselves. Other people can do cruel things that hurt us. We have no control over those events.

And yet we still have a choice about responsibility, choosing our ability to respond. We have a choice on how we will respond to any of those events that threaten us and our welfare. We have a choice in how we respond to events that can affect our future.

For just a moment, imagine yourself in a burning building. The flames are licking at the furniture around you. The heat is oppressive, the smoke clouding your vision.

If you are looking for fault, you may stand in the middle of the room and ask, "Who caused this fire? Whose fault is this? Somebody needs to be held accountable."

Or, you could choose to say; "I am getting myself and everyone else I can to safety. I will take it upon myself to get us out of here."

The first response is all about blame. The second is all about responsibility. Taking 100% responsibility for your life is saying, "Whatever comes my way, I will find the best way through it, to a better outcome."

About "Can't"

Moving out of reactivity and into the conscious intention to exercise 100% response-ability over our lives may sound like a daunting task. And truly, it does take time, determination, vigilance, and perseverance to accomplish—as well as a lot of self-forgiveness when we "blow it." But the pay-off in terms of personal freedom and equanimity is incredible.

So, it's important to remember that we are all a work in progress. And the work goes on throughout our lives because we are limitless in our potential to grow and because challenges are on-going.

When we fail to meet our own standards, or to rise to meet a challenge effectively, it's easy to shrug our shoulders and say, "Hey, I'm only human." But humans are endowed with the ability to respond to every situation—not perfectly—but in ever more effective ways. The key to unlocking this ability is our willingness to forgive ourselves and to learn from our mistakes.

A sure sign that somebody is choosing *not* to take full response-ability for their life is their use of the word "can't." I have noticed that there are actually four different "can'ts" that people employ.

First, "can't" may mean—it's not possible. And truly, there are physical limits that justify the use of that word. For example, I "can't" grow wings out of my shoulders. I "can't" breathe, unassisted, underwater. These are the physical limitations where something is simply not possible. These "can'ts" rarely get in our way. They are just the givens of life.

The second "can't" is when someone doesn't know how—they haven't acquired the knowledge to accomplish what needs to be done. It is a matter of gaining knowledge, learning skills, or changing strategies. For example, I "can't" be a doctor, as I don't know how. I don't have the skills or education. But I could pursue that, if I decided to.

The third "can't" is about timing. In that case, it may be that someone can't do something YET. A baby, for example, can't yet walk—it is not just a matter of learning a skill, but of the body developing to the point where it is possible. A child can't (yet) drive, as the child is simply not old enough. The "yet" of this "can't" will resolve in time.

But the fourth kind of can't is what gets us into trouble—the kind that means "won't." Someone might say, "I can't," but really means "I won't." For example, "I can't forgive that" is really "I won't forgive that." It is a choice, for whatever reason, to not move forward.

Just by changing our wording from "can't" to "won't," though, we actually assume response-ability for how we're feeling in the moment. And that's a great step forward from a place of feeling stuck in resistance or helplessness.

In truth, assuming response-ability isn't always about taking action. Sometimes, it's about being clear within ourselves and with others that we're *not* going to do something. We're not going to move ahead, pursue a relationship or a job opportunity, or whatever it is. But instead of being stuck in the "I can't"— which is all about, "I won't"—we're exercising our right and response-ability not to do something. "I won't" and "I will" are powerful statements that allow us to assume responsibility for what we do or what we choose not to do.

What is important here is clarity. "I can't" is a statement that robs you of both responsibility and potential. When you say, "I won't," you are claiming your own sense of power and choice. This creates a new clarity. It is, in essence, taking responsibility for a choice of NOT doing something. Not doing or doing, both are really about assuming response-ability.

As a coach and counselor, I've worked with many couples. And it's really quite amazing to see how quickly relationships start improving when one partner steps up and says, "I'm going to take responsibility for rebuilding our partnership."

This is not a declaration that this person is responsible for everything that's gone wrong in the relationship thus far. But from this point forward, this member of the couple is determined to do her or his best to help the relationship heal and improve. Thrivers look forward—not backward—with the intention of taking rational, responsible action in the present and future.

The Power of Self-Mastery

Change is a constant in life. We're not in control of unpredictable events, let alone the thoughts that run wild through our heads—most especially when we're under great stress. (We are responsible, however, for deciding how long we will hold on to those thoughts, once they enter our minds.)

If you think for a moment of all the things you wish you could control but can't, it's a very humbling experience. So, the bottom line is this: In the face of random events and unwanted changes and losses, we still have the power to exercise our Response Ability.

Unlike reactivity—which is rooted in fear—our response-ability is something we can develop and strengthen. The goal is to be able to discover and cultivate the hidden resources to respond to any situation with intelligence and heart.

This is no easy feat. But the truth is that even under stress and duress, as a seeming cyclone of thoughts and feelings threatens to overpower us, we can find a neutral place that is not swept away by the whirlwind. And this neutral witness is the part that can watch the mental and emotional reactivity without freaking out or taking physical action based upon it.

People who thrive know that a thought is just a thought, so they begin to deal with those thoughts differently by saying, "Okay, I'm having the thought of wanting to get revenge. I'm having the thought of wanting to do something really hurtful. But they're just thoughts. I don't have to act on them. I can allow these hurt feelings and angry thoughts to fade away. They do not define me and I won't allow them to confine me."

Remember, those feelings are a perfect barometer to the thoughts you are having. Those thoughts are just that—thoughts. They have no more power or control than what you assign them.

Again we can turn to Viktor Frankl's great work, *Man's Search for Meaning.* Clearly, there was nothing he could do to alter his situation as a prisoner in a Nazi concentration camp. All he could do in this hopeless situation was to exercise his response-ability by choosing to face the barbaric insanity with dignity, and to give his life meaning by being of service to those who needed comfort to endure the unendurable.

It would seem under such dire circumstances, that total despair was the only option. But Frankl—though he lost his wife and parents in the camps—found this not to be so.

Learning Response-Ability

Many people I've counseled feel blameless for their reactivity. It's just something that comes over them. An event happens that disturbs them greatly and they lash out in some way. I've had clients say to me, "Hey, what do you expect me to do? How do you expect me to feel? This is just how I am. I can't help it."

What I point out is that, yes, the response is automatic—it's a habit of thought and behavior. But it's also the reason why things haven't gotten any better. So although the conditioned, reflexive reaction is well entrenched, this doesn't mean it can't be changed—if the desire is there to do so.

So how do you gain leverage over an "automatic," reactive pattern that takes place faster than you can say, "OMG, I've done it again!"? Fortunately, it's simple (which is different than easy). It just takes strong intention and regular practice.

Step One: **Recognize that you have 100% response-ability**. No matter who you are or where you are or what's going on in your life—you have the power to strengthen your ability to respond in ways that are beneficial to everyone rather than detrimental to all.

Of course, it can sometimes take a moment to remember that. I recall standing in the parking lot, cursing at my car for the dead battery that went out sometime during lunch, while I was in the restaurant. How could that have happened to me, I wondered with great frustration and annoyance.

Then I remembered the couple of times when I turned the key in the ignition and the engine did not immediately engage. I was quite busy at the time and grateful that it did start, so I chose not to look upon that slight delay as the signal of an impending problem.

Clearly, I did not exercise my responsibility to take timely and corrective action. Now here I was, standing in the parking lot, cursing my car and my misfortune. While I waited for roadside service, I spent a little time forgiving myself for my negligence and committing myself to doing better next time. In the end, it was a defective battery. But I had several warnings that I chose to ignore.

When we're feeling angry, I think the first reaction is to look outside of ourself for where to place the blame. But in that split-second moment, before we point the finger of blame, we can breathe into our awareness that we carry the response-ability. This doesn't always mean that it's our fault. But it does always mean that we have the ability to respond rationally and compassionately.

I've heard partners in a relationship say, "I'm out of here. I'm done with this. I can't put up with it anymore so I'm leaving you." They put all the blame on the spouse for their having arrived at this decision. But like my momentary rage at my car for quitting on me, they may not be looking at all the ways they, themselves, neglected the relationship and all the things they could have done to heal it. And they may have ignored the signs along the way—those moments that may have tipped them off, had they been looking, that something was wrong.

Step Two: **Look for Ways to Take Responsibility**. One of the big truths of life is that we can't go back and change what's already happened—though we waste a lot of time and tears trying to do so. Only the present moment exists. And finding ways to exercise our response-ability Now is what will make the difference tomorrow.

Many of the people I counseled in the oncology ward of the hospital had a hard time getting to the place of deciding what to do next; they wanted to dwell on all that had happened that brought them to this place. That's an important life review process but not a great place to get stuck. I did my best to offer comfort, insight, and consolation. But my focus was to guide these cancer patients to ask the more productive questions like, "How can I move forward with this? How can I restore my relationships? How can I begin to take responsibility for where I go from here?"

I also talked with them about forgiveness—of self and others. This is an essential part of letting go of the past, so that we can begin again in the present. It's not something we do only once—but daily, every time we feel self-blame or blame of others. As we live more and more in the grace of our own forgiveness, we can become more and more responsible for changing the course of our lives.

We cannot change the past. It has happened. As we live into the present, we move toward the future. The past is about blame. In the present, we choose to be 100% responsible, so we can move into a better future.

Step Three: **Stay Aware of Your Thoughts and Redirect Them**. We are powerful beyond our own beliefs. But we can't exercise that power if we don't believe it's there.

Many people grow up with feelings that psychologist Martin Seligman has termed "learned helplessness." This is the belief that we can't exercise dominion over our own lives. And with that belief, we cede that power to care for ourselves to other people. And this disempowerment happens thought-by-thought-by-thought.

That's why it's so important to stay aware of our thoughts. How often do we tell ourselves "There's nothing I can do here. There's nothing I could've changed there"? It may be just background noise at this point, but it puts us into a trance of learned helplessness. What follows from that is "irresponsibility," which is to feel and act as if we are incapable of taking response-ability for our own lives.

When you're aware that these sorts of thoughts have captivated you, you can do a "pattern interrupt" by introducing an empowered scenario to counter the current thought. A friend of mine got very good at that—but not so good at the follow through. She'd feel incapable of dealing with what she perceived as a weakness in herself. But then she got good at making new resolutions for small action steps that could make a difference.

They definitely made a difference to how she felt in the moment. But then she got wise to the fact that her "learned hopefulness" was not enough to get her to follow through on her plans. She had to take the next step, which I call "learned determination." That's when you decide you're going to move forward, no matter what gets in your way.

You anticipate there will be obstacles and difficulties moving forward. You know you'll meet with your own resistance. But you make the commitment to yourself and determine to get to where you want to go because you know that it's important.

Step Four: **Review the Day—Every Day**. Reflecting on our intentions as we begin each day, and on our actions at the end of the day, is a beautiful way to stay current with and conscious of ourselves and of how we are doing on the path to becoming more responsible and fulfilled.

I recommend taking time for reflection before going to sleep, in which you ask yourself, "How did I take responsibility today? How did I shirk responsibility today? Where could I have been more response-able?" You might want to write down the answers to these questions so you can create new action steps to implement the next day.

Your daily life review is also a good time for writing in your Gratitude Journal (more on that in a bit). What a difference you can make to your day, to your sleep at night, and to the way your life unfolds in the times ahead with just a bit of self reflection, learned determination, and gratitude.

As the famous British Playwright, George Bernard Shaw said, "Life isn't about finding yourself. Life is about creating yourself." That's what we can do only when we take responsibility for ourselves. Choice by choice—as we grow more conscious and intentional—we have the power to become the very person we've been seeking. We can bring forth the inner greatness that resides in all our hearts. We can "create ourselves" day by day, moment by moment, by choosing our response and our response-ability.

We've all become so familiar with our human flaws and weaknesses. Yet, we've hardly begun to explore the strengths that are our birthright. We have no real sense of what our limitations are as human beings. We've held strong beliefs about what they are at various times, only to have someone come along and completely disprove them.

It usually takes a powerful challenge to help us discover that we're so much more than we ever thought we were. But when we consider what it takes to develop and maintain physical strength and fitness, we can better understand that life demands the same commitment of us on the mental and emotional levels if we are to maximize and actualize our greater potential for joy and fulfillment. The more we take responsibility for ourselves, the more we move into a thriving life.

TL;DR—Assume 100% Responsibility

- In every decision, we can make three choices. The first two are the automatic. The third is important. Any can be correct. But only when we choose intentionally. The three choices:
  1. Accept things as they are and continue on.
  2. Leave the situation.
  3. Change the situation, so that it works for all involved.
- The intentional choice makes an important shift for us, into responsibility. Taking responsibility for where life goes. Responsibility is different than blame. Blame is looking for who is at fault. Responsibility is looking at how to shift to a better place.
- E + R = O. Viktor Frankl and Jack Canfield both point to the fact that there is always a choice in Response. The E is the Event. Something happens in life. It is not the same as the O—"Outcome." The difference is in the R—"Response" each person can choose. Your response does not equal the outcome, but your response can shift the outcome. That *response* is the start of choosing *Responsible*—the ability to respond.
- When a challenge comes along, there is no help in asking, "Whose fault is this?" If a house is burning, asking "Who started this fire?" does little. Instead, taking responsibility to move to a safe place, and working to ensure the safety of others, is the better option. That is the shift from blame to responsibility.
- The steps to Responsibility are:
  1. Recognize you have 100% response-ability. You have the power of choosing your response in any situation, even if that is only the choice of attitude.
  2. Look for ways to take responsibility.
  3. Stay aware of your thoughts (and remember, "a thought is just a thought").
  4. Review your day, every day. Commit to responsibility.

Chapter 6

show up

"The present moment, if you think about it, is the only time there is. No matter what time it is—it is always now."
—Marianne Williamson

I had an unforgettable experience in Las Vegas a few years ago. And it's not what you're thinking.

Yes—I did enter the casino—but I'm not much of a gambler. I was attending a conference in the hotel with its intentional architectural design that has all pathways intersect through the casino.

As you can imagine, the casino was a sensory assault. It was filled with smoke, lit-up like Christmas, and loud with incessant, nerve-jangling electronic noises. I've been in casinos before—on a cruise ship and on other trips to Las Vegas for conferences. But this one really grabbed my attention.

Ironically, the subject of the conference was finding your purpose in life and living it fully in the world. The contrast between this focus and that of the people seeking pleasure (and perhaps wealth) in the casino couldn't have been more striking. Both groups were investing in their future. But the one in the casino was staking it all on the roll of the dice, the play of a card, or the lucky pull of a lever. The ones at the conference were following a tried-and-true path to success: creating intentions, setting goals, forming strategic alliances, and taking appropriate action steps.

The first thing I noticed about the recreational gamblers was that their eyes looked glazed over—like no one was really home. They reminded me, alarmingly, of old-fashioned mechanical toys that repeat the same action over and over again—once they are all wound up. And these people were definitely wound up.

Those in front of the slots would pull the lever and watch the spin, take a drag on their cigarette, take a sip of their drink, plug in some more money, then pull the lever again—and again, and again. It was like watching a room full of sleepwalkers who were dreaming they were awake. Of course not everyone behaved this way. But almost all of them did, which is why I'm sharing this experience with you now.

I wandered back to the conference room, feeling a bit shaken. "Do you believe in zombies?" I asked the person in the chair next to me. He looked at me strangely—certain that this was a trick question. So, I said, "Really. Do you believe that zombies exist?"

He wrinkled his forehead and said, "No. Of course not. What are you talking about?"

"Well, it's interesting," I told him. "I just saw a whole bunch of zombies together in one room."

He was taken aback, and at first, must have thought I'd seen a room full of movie extras waiting for their time on camera. So, I quickly clarified that the empty-eyed people I was referring to were the ones in the casino who were lost in the mindless activity of smoking, drinking, and pulling the lever.

While their bodies were there, they were not Showing Up.

Living in the Present

Gambling in Las Vegas looks a lot different than it looks in the commercials. In place of sophisticated people risking a few bucks to pay for a good time, most of the people I encountered were neither thriving nor present in the moment. They weren't laughing and celebrating, like in the commercials. They were somber and glazed.

Even when they won a jackpot, they didn't seem to come to life for more than an instant. Then it was back to pulling, and puffing, and sipping, and plugging more money into the slots in hopes of an even bigger payoff. They were addicted to the process and the emotional highs and lows that go with it. All the noise and lights just served to deepen their trance.

At the conference I was attending, people were expectant and somewhat excited. They were conversing meaningfully with each other, making eye contact, friendships, and business connections. The whole room was energized because everyone shared the intention of moving forward in very practical ways. It was not the kind of artificial frenzy of the casino.

If you walk through a casino, you'll notice that there are no windows. There are no clocks. The people who run them want you to lose track of time, to mix night and day, and to literally lose yourself in the experience. If you're numb to the losses you're incurring financially—but still dreaming that the next pull of the lever could turn everything around—you'll be motivated to keep going, and going, and going.

Being fully present in the moment is a timeless experience—while disappearing into an endless series of repetitious actions is the exact opposite. I couldn't help but think of donkeys hitched to a millstone, perpetually moving forward to catch up with the carrot dangling in front of their noses. Meanwhile, their meaningless motion grinds the grain that enriches the millionaire casino owners.

Occasionally, of course, there is a big winner! There'd have to be to keep everyone else endlessly pulling the levers like trained mice seeking small rewards. But as we all know by now about most big lottery winners, within a few years most are broke again and probably friendless. After the money is gone, the "party" goes elsewhere.

Showing Up in the Moment

No doubt you've heard this statement from Woody Allen, "Eighty percent of success is showing up." But what exactly does that mean?

As my experience in the casino amply demonstrates, being physically present but mentally absent really doesn't qualify. To my way of thinking, Showing Up means being present—in body, mind, and spirit—and responding with conscious intention and awareness to each new moment.

That's not easy to do—most especially when the moment is painful and difficult. When the going gets tough, many tune out and dive into distractions rather than face the challenges head on.

When asked in an interview what he meant by his 80% statement, Woody Allen said, in effect, "If you want to be a good violinist—you have to show up to practice, and you have to show up to perform. You can't just say, 'I want to be a great violinist,' and then do nothing to get there. You have to show up repeatedly for the process to become a great violinist."

Over the last eight years, my family has established a New Year's Eve tradition in which we each pick a word that describes a quality we desire to embody in the coming year. A couple of years ago, I chose, "Show-Up." (And I readily admit that I cheated, hyphenating two words, so I could follow the rule of choosing one word.) I set the intention to do that every day of the new year, to truly Show Up.

During that year, I asked myself every morning, "How do I want to show up today?" And each evening, I asked myself, "How am I showing up? How am I being truly present with people? How am I being a full participant in life and not just going through the motions?"

While I was not perfect, I certainly showed up to life much more that year—and I made it a habit.

Dealing with What Gets in the Way

Of course, no sooner had I set that positive intention then I became aware of all the inner voices and outer obstacles that make it so hard to show up in each moment. Fortunately, now that I've devoted a substantial period of time to encountering and surmounting such obstacles, I've found a handy way to categorize the types of distractions I kept encountering. You might find this useful, too. For convenience sake, I've named these distractions "The Three T's." They are Thoughts, Tasks, and Technology.

Thoughts: The incessant mind chatter that we call "thinking" only poses a problem when we actually listen to it. Of course, it's easier *not to* take an interest in a thought when we're not feeling stressed out. But even when we are, it's helpful to stay aware of the fact that probably 95% of those incessant thoughts that are so "full of sound and fury"—really do signify nothing. Holding this as a general truth can make it easier to turn our focus elsewhere—as many times a day as is required to stay in balance.

As we all know, ruminations about the past or worries about the future can totally preoccupy us—while the present drains away moment-by-moment. Interestingly, thoughts are rarely about this moment. They are about what has happened (the past) and what might happen (the future). Focusing on what did or didn't happen in the past can lead to depression while worrying about the future can create anxiety.

When we let the thoughts inside our head become our momentary reality, the words someone else is speaking to us can get drowned out by the cacophony of our internal voices. We may look like we're present with that other person. But all they're really getting of us is the shell of who we are. The rest is swept away by our busy thoughts and the waves of emotion that arise from them. We've literally gotten carried away with our own thoughts and have missed what could have been a meaningful exchange with another person.

Those thoughts can continuously plague us with inner conflict and criticism. Being present in the moment is actually our only "safety zone." For when we notice a thought as only a thought, we realize that nothing else exists but the moment. Everything else is a highly charged fantasy we've been creating for ourselves, which diminishes our capacity to function efficiently in the moment.

One technique for returning to this moment—following a temporary voyage out into the realms of the imagination—is to become conscious of our breath and to slow it down. Another is to focus on sensations—sounds, fragrances, tastes, touch, sights—occurring within and around us.

Tasks are another way we can leave the present behind. It's easy to get caught up with the little things that are, in the end, of little importance. Maybe a spouse needs to connect with you—or your children want to tell you about their day at school or camp. Instead, we feel compelled to stay busy with something that could actually wait. It's not that those tasks aren't worthwhile. It's just that they're not worth as much as moments in communion with someone important to us who needs our time and attention.

Of course, we can't talk about distractions and tasks without also mentioning multi-tasking. Many people believe themselves capable of doing a number of things at the same time. However, research indicates that dividing our attention doesn't actually multiply our effectiveness. Research consistently shows that it diminishes it. And have you ever tried to hold a meaningful conversation with someone whose mind is focused elsewhere? It's not a very satisfying experience.

Then, there is **technology**. We have endless electronic options for being in many places at once. Observing people out together—each absorbed in their own separate world—is one of the strange and unfortunate phenomena of instant global connectivity. While the whole world is at our fingertips that which is closest to us can sometimes seem the furthest away.

In no way am I stating that you need to ditch your technology. I have a smartphone in my pocket and a tablet nearby most of the time. And I have been involved on the Internet with several websites since 2000. But I do appreciate that there is a time and a place for technology—and more importantly, a time and a place to leave it alone.

AWOL: Absent Without Leaving

For most adults, Showing Up in the moment takes a strong intention and concerted practice to get back to what is natural for us as children. Watch a two-year enjoy an ice cream cone and you'll remember what present moment awareness actually looks like. As we get older, it's so easy for us to get distracted by Thoughts, Tasks, and Technology.

The need to find the still, quiet center in the midst of the frenzy—whether that frenzy is occurring within or outside of us or both—has made "mindfulness meditations" almost mainstream today. As the world speeds up and our issues gather steam, being able to slow down and show up as our best self in each moment is an art worth cultivating. Without becoming mindful, we can easily cheat ourselves out of the fullness of life's most poignant moments. We also prevent the people around us from connecting more deeply with us. And such connections enrich life for everyone.

Of course, sometimes it feels a whole easier to simply float through life—or zone out in some way—like the people in the casino. You might know people who have basically gone lazily through their life, without ever really showing up for it. But if not showing up reduces awareness of the pain, it also reduces the pleasures and gain available to us in life.

All Present & Accounted For

Showing up means that we are physically, emotionally, and spiritually present. We're aware of how our body feels. We're watching our thoughts and feelings. We're also connected with our spiritual core, which gives us a deeper sense of our purpose in the world.

The difference in our quality of life when we're all present and accounted for is more striking than the difference between watching a film in black and white and watching it in full color and 3-D. Just think of what it's like to sit down with someone dear to you—to look into that person's eyes—and listen to them fully, not only with your ears but also with your presence. By so doing, you also allow them to experience you in your fullness in the moment. Then, regardless of whether you're feeling joy or sorrow, this deep connection with another person is deeply healing for you both. It is a truly authentic interaction that has lasting impact on your lives and serves as a point of reference for what feels most nourishing when relating to another.

Fully showing up in the moment, however, doesn't even require that another person be present. Here's what I mean:

Often, when I go out for a run on a trail near my home, I often do so with my headphones on. Sometimes, however, I recognize the need to take those headphones off and become aware and immersed in all that surrounds me.

I feel the Earth underneath my feet, the breeze on my face, the sweat running down my back, my pulse throbbing in me. I feel what it's like to hit those leaves as I rush by, to feel the tickle of sticky spider webs, to run through the creek across the rocks. When this happens, I feel so much more vitally alive. I recognize how much more invigorating this run feels than when I'm just trying to get in some exercise while distracting myself from the tedium of it. When I run with awareness, I'm really present in a wholly different way. I'm showing up for myself. And I feel inextricably connected to the natural world around me. Then, when I rejoin the human world, I am more present for this experience, as well.

How to Show-Up in the Moment

The first step is to set an intention of showing up. Just deciding that you are going to show up more creates a shift. When I chose "Show-Up" for my word that year, I had a note at the top of my calendar every day that said, "Show Up." It was a daily reminder to be intentional.

And each day, after noting my intention, I would take a quick inventory on how I was doing. Each meal made a good time to just do a quick check. Before bedtime, I did a review of where I had (and had not) "shown up" that day, with a new intention to do better the next day.

The second step, of course, is to be aware of the distractions—and avoid them when they get in the way of something more important. The 3 T's—Thoughts, Tasks, and Technology—all can have value when handled judiciously. We can choose to pay no mind to the annoying inner noise that interferes with meaningful interactions. We can set our thoughts aside and really listen to the other person without planning our rebuttal before they're even finished speaking.

We can limit the time we spend on our electronic devices and then carefully choose when it is that we spend that time. The possibility of falling down the rabbit hole into the intricate, seemingly infinite realm of the Internet is a peril all of us face every day and must skillfully navigate. A friend sends us an interesting article, we click a link to another—that then leads to many others. In no time, too much time has disappeared into the ethers with nothing significant to show for it.

Put a cap on it. Allow yourself some indulgence but limit it to what works best in your situation.

The third step is to confront our fears. According to Ralph Waldo Emerson, "He who is not everyday conquering some fears has not learned the secret of life." As we've already discussed, fear can be a protector but is more often a preventer of our advancement toward greater self-expression and fulfillment. It also feels the same in the body as excitement. So when the fear comes up, give yourself some time to discover what it's really saying to you so you can take advantage of this important sensory signal. To show up is to feel the fear, understand it is not necessarily about avoidance, and realize it is only telling you to pay attention.

The fourth step is to practice forgiveness. This step requires that we resolve the issue with another person that left us feeling hurt and resentful. We have to show up to forgive, and we have to forgive to show up fully. So this is a process with several small, interconnected steps. When taken one-by-one, they can ultimately lead to a deepening of our connection with another person or the wise realization that it is best to go our separate ways—at least for now.

The fifth step to showing up is committing to being present. As I just described, when I go out for a run "unplugged," then I'm present and available to witness and experience the unexpected. I get to see "ordinary" things with extraordinary awareness that actually heightens my enjoyment.

Being present to our own experience requires that we stay more awake and aware of the data constantly being sent by our senses to our brain. By so doing, we realign with ourselves, which allows us to show up ready and able to deal with whatever comes up next.

The sixth step is to offer yourself in service to another person. By listening to someone without any agenda or attempt to convince them of anything else, we give a gift that is rare in the world: The time and intention to see that person clearly, to hear them fully, and to understand what it's like to be them. That alone can make an enormous positive difference in their life.

I have this distinct memory of working with a group of teenagers. I was watching two of them interact and noticed something peculiar: neither was listening to the other. Both people would be having a conversation, but they were not going back-and-forth. Each was just continuing his or her monologue. There was no listening. Just speaking.

Deep listening pulls us into the present moment. So many conversations are really two-way monologues disguised as a dialogue. Yet, nothing new is really learned by either party from that so-called exchange. It's when we show up and listen intently to another person that we hear not only the substance of what they're saying, but also the feelings they have about what they are describing.

Having just one other person who "gets" us—in the moment and just as we are—is enough to help us become more fully okay about who we are. And with that other person's acknowledgement, acceptance, and "permission," it's easier to show up more fully in life. I believe that giving and receiving such a gift is part of what it means to fully engage in the human experience.

The Four P's

Someone I know who had a very challenging life used to live by this motto, "Wake me when it's over." She went through the motions of what she thought she had to do in life. Finally, after quite a few years, she awoke to the fact that she really didn't have to do any of it. From then on, she was able to find the emotional, psychological, and spiritual support she needed to continually awaken to ever-greater degrees of inner freedom and awareness on the journey back home to herself.

Life is a perilous journey. We never really know what we're going to be challenged to face in the very next moment. That's why showing up fully is so important for thriving—so that we have all our resources available to deal with whatever occurs.

In that year that I focused so intently on showing up, I found it enormously helpful to develop a habit of reflecting each night on how well I did during the day. I highly recommend this practice.

Here are the questions I use in my self-inquiry

- Where did I show up?
- Where did I fail to show up fully?
- What are the ways that I avoided showing up?
- What kept me from showing up more fully?
- Was it a distraction?

- If so, how did I distract myself?
  - ○ Was it laziness?
  - ○ Was it fear?
  - ○ Was I harboring resentment?
- When was I less fully my Authentic Self?
- How did I shirk away from my true self to become something else and less that that?
- Why did that happen?

I don't interrogate myself when I go through this inquiry. I just reflect with compassion and with the intention of being more fully present in the moment. I never expect to perform perfectly. Progress is not an arrow pointing straight upward. It's a zigzagging line of steady effort toward a goal that will always be a little bit beyond me. And that's where the 4 Powerful P's come into play.

The first P is about **Presence**, which requires that we endeavor to show up authentically in the moment and in the world. Unfortunately, few people actually do that these days—given the desire and opportunities to numb out to all our problems. That's why just holding the intention to be Present in the moment—even if we fall short by our own estimation—can transform how we begin to interact with the people around us.

The second P is about **Purpose**. Discovering what it is that make us feel most alive—and then regularly pursuing that as a way to positively impact our world—makes it far easier to show up fully, despite whatever else is going on in our lives. Living for a purpose larger than the satisfaction of our personal needs is an important ingredient for showing up and staying present in the world.

The third P is for **Passion**, which entails living with the greater sense of aliveness that purpose gives to us. Dedicating our lives to the full expression of our being—doing what we love and being of service in the world as a consequence— not only makes us feel more vital, it also functions like shock absorbers that give us some immunity to the threat of being jolted off- course by every bump along the way. Purpose and passion often go hand-in-hand.

While Purpose is almost always tied to something greater than ourselves, passion can also include involvement in activities that we love. I won't change the world by paddle boarding, Scuba diving, or trail running. But the recharge it gives me in the pursuit of those passions allows me to give more to the passions I have that lead to a sense of purpose.

Lastly, what we need is **Patience**—with ourselves and with each other. After all, we're going to have times when we find ourselves distracted, lazy, fearful, and resentful. At such times, berating ourselves creates only guilt and remorse. Remember, those critical voices are thoughts. And as we have touched upon repeatedly, a thought is just a thought. You don't have to buy into those chastising voices. Offer yourself patience, as a "project in progress."

Notice that there is one P missing: Perfection. This is not about being perfect, but being human. But FULLY human, connected with others and with yourself. You won't make perfection, but you can certainly increase the amount of time you Show Up.

What we need is patience and compassionate self-forgiveness. Only then are we able to show up ever more fully and live with passion and vitality. When we practice this regularly, we become a conduit of blessings that helps many others to awaken and become more fully alive.

 TL;DR—Show Up

- When you Show Up, you are engaged in life and with those around you. You are "in the present" and "in the presence," giving your own "presence" to the world.
- There are several barriers to showing up:
  1. Thoughts. The constant chatter of our minds keeps us distracted—many times, our conversations are even dominated with our minds racing to decide how next to respond.
  2. Tasks. Many times, the unimportant tasks crowd us out of our own lives. We get so busy with the mundane that we miss the important task of showing up, to ourselves and with others. The truly important is lost to the incessant unimportant.
  3. Technology. So many devices can keep us focused, head down, on a screen. We aren't, then, heads up, focused on life.
- Here's how to Show Up more in the moment:
  1. Make it your intention to show up. The decision to do this makes a shift in your outlook and approach.
  2. Be aware of your distractions. Choose how you will set the distractions aside.
  3. Confront the fears. Sometimes, our fears keep us a bit removed from really interacting and truly showing up.
  4. Practice forgiveness. If you have resentments with someone, it is difficult to choose to show up with that person in your presence.
  5. Commit to being present. Practice living in the present moment. Living in the past or the future keeps you from showing up in the current moment.
  6. Offer yourself in service. Listen with no agenda. Give the other person the present of your presence, truly listening and responding.
- Reflect on your process each day. Showing Up is a skill to be practiced. Reflect on how your 4 P's are going:
  1. Presence.

2. Purpose.
3. Passion.
4. Patience

Chapter 7

practice gratitude

"When we focus on our gratitude, the tide of disappointment goes out and the tide of love rushes in."
—Kristin Armstrong

"I don't have to chase extraordinary moments to find happiness—it's right in front of me if I'm paying attention and practicing gratitude."
—Brene Brown

"Gratitude is not only the greatest of virtues, but the parent of all the others."
—Marcus Tullius Cicero

g ratitude can save your life! But like turning a sailboat around in a squall, it can take enormous strength and effort to find something to appreciate when the winds of change are literally clearing the decks, rocking the boat, and threatening to totally capsize you. That's why it's so essential to develop the muscle and mindset of gratefulness, the state of gratitude, every day, even and especially when the winds appear to be blowing you off the course you set for your life.

Then there are those times when we feel completely becalmed at sea and unable to make any headway towards our destination—despite our most strenuous efforts. Here, too, gratitude can keep us upright (instead of uptight) and forbearing while we await a change in the weather.

Seen in this perspective, gratitude is so much more than a social nicety or obligation we exchange in conversation. It is a lever by which we turn the powerfully creative force of our attention from a focus on what is missing in our life or what is going "wrong," to appreciating what is still present—and trusting the value of what is to come.

So much of life really does come down to mood and attitude. The mind, like gravity, can pull us into a downward spiral. Gratitude gives us altitude—allowing us to see our troubles in the context of the Bigger Picture. And since we get more of what we focus on, by assessing and appreciating the good in any situation, we open ourselves to the Better.

Thanks for Nothing

Recently, I went to the Dominican Republic with a small team to help work on a building project. One of the things that really struck me about the people we met was how open, friendly, and genuinely happy they seemed. They didn't have much to their name—in fact, barely enough to get by. But the relationships between the people in the village where we stayed appeared to be very rich and satisfying to them. There was even a sense that whatever challenges anyone had to face, they had a whole community of people behind them to face it with them.

Now, I'm not trying to paint an idealized portrait of contented yet impoverished village folk. because it was far from that. But there were definitely elements in the way these people related to their lives and to each other that I think we can learn from.

Not long ago, a friend of mine asked some visitors from South America whether they aspired to live in the U.S. The response was instantaneous. "No way!" one of them said to her. "You're all too busy to enjoy your lives."

The relative simplicity of life for the people in the village where we were, and their level of appreciation, seemed to buoy their spirits and brighten their countenance in spite of the hardships and deprivations they faced. By contrast, many people with a lot more stuff seem a lot less happy.

While it is not necessarily a side-effect of accumulation, I have noticed that many with much struggle to experience gratitude. Accumulation often becomes something of an addiction, with a hidden belief that "just a little bit more" will lead to joy and contentment.

Too Much of a Good Thing

Today, most ordinary people in the U.S. and Europe live with greater abundance and convenience than did even the super-rich of an earlier era. We are so enormously privileged. And yet without appreciation, there is no real or lasting enjoyment.

As someone pointed out to me years ago, "How quickly privileges become rights." Just as soon as we believe that we're entitled to what we have—and to what we want—we sacrifice the very thing we need to be able to enjoy all our privileges and possessions. Have you heard the saying, "If you've forgotten the language of gratitude, you'll never be on speaking terms with happiness"?

So many of us get so caught up in doing more in order to have more, to outshine others, and to provide more for our families that we forget to experience the joy that gratitude generates when we take a little time to acknowledge and appreciate all that we already have. Stoking the fires of our desires for more than we really need or can possibly enjoy are the marketing departments of countless manufacturers.

We're bombarded by words and images meant to persuade us that by purchasing one product or another, we will smell better, feel better, look better, have more, be more successful and become one of the "beautiful" people living an enviable life. After a certain age, we rationally know it's essentially bogus—yet the possibilities are so attractive and the advertising so seductive that we often choose to forget.

The only problem with all this is that there never seems to be a stopping point where we finally achieve satisfaction and a feeling of "enoughness"—at least not so long as we equate our happiness and value with anything outside ourselves. This is what often happens when we don't regularly practice gratitude for what we already have.

Freedom from Want

I remember a classic line I read years ago in a book review that said something like—"The U.S. is the only country in which being adequate was not enough." Needless to say, this is now true for much of the industrialized world.

There's ironic humor in this. How could adequate be inadequate? Yet, when I looked up the word in an on-line dictionary, the first meaning given was "sufficient" and the second meaning was "barely sufficient."

So many of us grow up feeling barely sufficient—like we, ourselves, just don't make the grade. A friend of mine calls this feeling the "not-enuff stuff." We believe we're not attractive enough, smart enough, rich enough, lucky enough. You name it and we think we're just not enough of whatever "It" is; or that we just don't have enough of what it takes to be really happy and successful.

Bernie Madoff is the "poster child" for this maddening dilemma, which turned his prosperous life into a classic Greek Tragedy. His inability to satisfy his ravenous appetite for "enuffness"—and to abide in a state of gratefulness for all that he and his family already possessed—created at least $18 billion in losses for the thousands of investors who entrusted their life savings to him. Some of these people then took their own lives—including one of Madoff's sons.

This leaves us with the question—how can we attain "Freedom from Want" and experience a sense of sufficiency in our lives? The practice of appreciation offers one essential answer to this question.

It is often not a matter of how much one has, but how little we may feel we have. The level of wealth is less important than the feelings associated with not having more.

It's interesting how we describe money as "appreciating" when it grows in "interest." We could almost say the same thing about ourselves: When we grow more interested in counting and appreciating all the blessings we already have, we also grow—in our level of life satisfaction. We grow in appreciation.

What I observed about the people in the Dominican Republic was that they were very wealthy with gratitude and appreciation for their lives and for each other. And these two very potent emotions have self-healing, mood-enhancing properties.

For me this underscores the truth that thriving has a lot more to do with our mindset than it does our circumstances. And appreciating what we have—even and especially during difficult times—is one of the most enriching habits that we, as Thrivers, can ever cultivate.

A good place to start is with appreciation for oneself—for all our qualities, experiences, achievements—and even for our shortcomings. With greater self-appreciation—along with compassionate self-forgiveness for being less than perfect—we can more readily appreciate our families, friends, communities, and the beauty of the world in which we live.

From there, we can nurture gratitude for those around us. Start with the easy ones—those we love and with whom we share a connection. Next, we can have a greater sense of gratitude for those who make our world a better place. As our heart starts feeling more full—which it will, the more authentically grateful we feel—we can even practice gratitude for those whom we find more "challenging." Many times, those challenges lead us to growth and development.

In working with broken marriages, I suggest that the person working with me practice gratitude toward the fact that the other spouse (almost always the one who announced they had a problem) even brought the issues of the marriage to the foreground. I suggest my clients thank their spouse for waking them up to how things had become. That place of gratitude sets the stage for rebuilding.

Once gratitude starts to become automatic—not as a ritual but as a genuine moment of reflection and appreciation—the momentum generated by the powerful force of the gratitude habit can keep us afloat even in stormy weather. It may even awaken us to appreciate what we'd normally consider barely enough, allowing us to shift from striving to thriving.

How Sweet It Is!

An amazing adventurous woman I know told me the other day about moments of extreme gratitude she has had—which were heightened by the periods of deprivation that preceded them. She was at a silent meditation retreat for 10 days in an ashram in Indonesia when the experience she shared with me occurred.

There was no speaking at the retreat. There was also no eye contact made. Therefore, there was no one to dilute the intensity of this woman's full-on experience of her own tumultuous thoughts and feelings.

The first meal of the day was at 4:30 a.m. and was tasty, vegan, and quite minimal. Dinner was at 11:00 a.m. And the final snack—a bowl of fruit—was at 4:30 pm.

The weather was sweltering—day and night. Though they'd been warned of pythons seeking the cool tiles of the bathroom floor to sleep on at night, she chose to take her chances with the snakes as those bathroom tiles were the only place where she, too, could cool off. So she slept naked on the tiles, drenching her sarong in water to drape over herself as she slept.

One afternoon, she sat before her final meal of the day—a bowl of fruit with coconut sprinkles—and broke down in tears of gratitude. She wept for how beautiful the fruit appeared to her and how blessed she was that she was not starving—as so many people in the world are.

The rawness of her feelings made her deeply empathic to the plight of the destitute. She realized that great gratitude often doesn't show up until we are confronted with the absence of something very precious to us.

This same woman told me about her dentist. Because she spends time in other countries, when she came to see him recently after a considerable period of time she was shocked to discover that he'd become a quadriplegic. He told her he'd been struck by a driver while riding his bike in Santa Monica a few years back.

The dentist still comes into the office to book appointments with his clients and converse with them. The dentist who took over his practice does the actual dental work. The woman is in awe at what a kind and compassionate man he has become in the process of enduring this dramatic change in his life. "I hope I don't have to go through something really awful to be more grateful," she said to me. He is proof, though, that any challenge includes an opportunity for gratitude.

In an earlier chapter I mentioned my experience as a hospital chaplain in the oncology ward of a hospital. Most of the people I met were walking the thin line between life and death. And they did so with such a clear awareness and heightened appreciation for what is most important to them in their life.

Normally, there's so much clutter and busyness in daily life—so it can be hard to discern what's truly meaningful among all that is fighting for our attention. But when illness strikes, our priorities suddenly get very clear. We become laser-focused on what is truly important, and conversely, on what is not.

A lot of the conversations I had with the patients on the ward sounded something like this—"I'm so grateful that I'm now awake. I'm so grateful to realize all that I have in my life. I've operated under the assumption that I didn't have enough. And now that I'm facing this huge illness, I realize that there were beautiful things to be grateful for all along. I'm so fortunate to finally be seeing that."

Nobody on the oncology ward ever told me that they were glad they got sick. But many were grateful to their illness for waking them up. I've since met several women who said that the cancer they faced and overcame was the best thing that ever happened to them because it led them to change their entire approach and direction to life. That was my experience, too, when I was ill. Suddenly, I became painfully aware of the fact that I'd been letting my life fly by—almost as if without me.

Appreciation as the Antidote to Deprivation

When we're hurting and feeling the lack of what we're sure will make us happier— health, money, love, success, a child, a cruise, etc.—hearing that a change of attitude will give us greater altitude in our worldview seems like a poor substitute for the real thing. It may also make us feel that we're meant to settle for less and be grateful for what we have when there's still so many unmet needs in our lives. But if what we need isn't present for us now, what can we do to alleviate our angst over its absence?

The answer, of course, is to take stock of what we already have that we have likely taken for granted as a "given." Something deeply desired in the past and now a part of our present, can fade into the background of our awareness like wallpaper. We expect it to be there rather than appreciate that it is. Yet appreciation can keep things fresh and alive in our awareness and can elevate our mood and spirits.

Over the years of working with couples struggling in their relationship, I have watched them focus on "what is not" and miss the "what is." Many who struggled with fertility became so focused on what they did not have that they starved the relationship with their spouse, which they did have. For some, this awareness came too late.

One woman I know confessed to me, "I feel I deserve all the blessings in my life—but not the hardships." That's the ultimate stance for never finding happiness or contentment. It turns a person into an entitled victim.

Taking the time to enjoy and appreciate what we have rather than enumerating and lamenting what we don't have can turn the glass from "half empty" to "half full." By placing our focus on presence rather than absence, we generate feelings of pleasure and contentedness in ourselves. And when we make this a daily practice—and are able to sustain a predominantly positive disposition, we actually re-set our mind and brain.

Study after study affirms the power of gratitude to shift our brain function, shift our mood, and move us toward a lower stress response. New research shows that the habit of gratitude creates permanent changes in the neuronal structure in our brain. And this also reflects in changes of the Amygdala, the part of the brain responsible for our threat/fear reaction.

True Confession

With all these positive benefits, you'd think that being grateful was a "no-brainer." But that's the whole problem: We have a brain—and it often gets in our way.

Especially when we're feeling fear, our mind can hijack our attention, lure us down a dark alley, and "mug" us with scary stories of negative possibilities that send stress hormones racing through our bodies. So, here's what you need to know about me: I'm not immune to this danger.

As conscientious as I try to be about practicing gratitude—and appreciating what I do have rather than worrying about what I don't—this is definitely an area where I constantly need reminding. There are times when I start to get anxious that there's not going to be enough or that things aren't going to work out as

I had hoped and planned. If I don't catch and redirect my mind right away, then in no time, it's manufacturing frightening scenarios and uncomfortable neurochemicals that impede my ability to take constructive action.

So what do I do if it gets this far? I remember to take a few deep breaths, take a couple of mental steps back, and then shift my focus to how fortunate I really am. It's a brief "time-out" during which I take a quick inventory of what I do have and who I have become: the health of my body, family, and coaching practice; opportunities to experience wider perspectives; moments of beauty that are around me waiting to be noticed; and even sunshine on my shoulders.

A few minutes focused on the blessings in my life helps me to reestablish my sense of gratitude and appreciation. Once I'm there, everything starts to look better—or at least to feel more manageable.

What Good Is It To Be Grateful?

There is a lot of research now proving that gratitude enhances personal well-being. So, while we can point to the value of being grateful from a psychological, philosophical, and/or religious perspective, what's even more persuasive is the science that demonstrates the positive impact on our biology and emotional life that we generate when we are grateful.

Just by viewing our lives through the eyes of gratitude, allowing that feeling to seep into our hearts, and then giving voice to it—through our speaking or writing—we boost the dopamine load in our brain. We move away from fear and defensiveness into a greater sense of happiness, optimism, joy, pleasure, and enthusiasm for life. It's better than any medication we could possibly take, as the more grateful we are, the less depressed we feel.

Along with the reduction in anxiety, blood pressure, and depression, gratitude also gives a boost to our immune system. People who are grateful also tend to sleep better because they're focused on feeding the positive feelings rather than allowing the fear to feed on their imaginations in their dreams.

Gratitude enhances our emotional resilience. It can be like a lifeline we throw to ourselves when we feel that we're drowning in our sorrows and difficulties. The more we're able to savor the pluses rather than tally and bemoan the minuses, the greater the strength of our resilience. And, by expressing our appreciation to others, we stimulate oxytocin—the connection hormone—in us all.

Part of the Thriver's task is to build new neuronal pathways by focusing on gratitude. We train our brain to stay away from its negative bias by developing an automatic tendency to see and appreciate the positive aspects even in difficult situations.

Gratitude Overcomes Gravity

Negativity carries a mental gravitational energy that pulls us downward into misery. In the survival of the fittest, by which the human brain was shaped, it was the pessimists who won, for they were the ones expecting danger behind every rock and bush, and in every tree and cave.

Today, most of us are still operating on high alert—over-reacting to the wildly over-stimulating and completely confusing environment of ever-accelerating change in which we now live. Day and night, a ceaseless stream of mental commentary is flowing through the airwaves and the channels of our minds often heightening our stress.

One of my friends told me that when chaos is reigning—inside and out—she declares her mind "a crime scene" and visualizes yellow police tape surrounding it so she remembers *not* to tune-in to whatever it is she's thinking. She's knows in that moment that her thoughts are "out of order" and could only cause her more angst—at least until she finds a way to bring herself back into balance.

Of course, she's not alone. That's why meditation has gone mainstream—to help us watch and transcend the mind so that its default programming doesn't interfere with our optimal functioning.

While not everyone feels they can set aside time to meditate, anyone can train their brain to focus on positive experiences. We can do this by frequently reminding ourselves to think of someone or something we really enjoy and then consciously generate feelings of appreciation for them.

That's what Thrivers do: When misery-making thoughts start damming the flow of good feelings, they survey the landscape of their mind or environment for people and places to appreciate. They know that this also helps them find the good that's present even in painful situations.

Changing Poison Into Medicine

Some years ago I worked in an environment where promises were made to me but not kept. My rising levels of frustration, bitterness, and animosity toward the owner of the office created a toxic internal environment for me.

Fortunately, it didn't take too long for me to catch on to what I was doing to myself. And once I saw that this situation wasn't healthy for me—outwardly or inwardly—I did several simple but important things that those who aspire to thrive strive to practice as often as needed.

First, I changed my attitude. I think that's always the best place to start—because it's the only thing we can control in a situation like that. A change of attitude also gives us the opportunity to contemplate how it is that we've gotten into such a situation. There may be something to learn from that inquiry.

Next, I chose to take total responsibility for being in this circumstance—and staying in it as long as I did. I know from experience that only by doing so can I possibly create change. Otherwise, I could end up feeling like a helpless victim being taken advantage of by an unfair boss.

Then, I focused on the value I derived from being there. In this case, it was primarily a paycheck. But it was also the motivation to take effective action—which is what I ultimately did. I looked for better situations and soon found a succession of opportunities that led to where I am today. Had there not been a "burr under my saddle," or something equivalent to the grain of sand that annoys an oyster, I might still be wasting away at a so-so job that wasn't nearly as fulfilling as what I'm doing now.

Looking back—with great gratitude for where I am now in my life—I can also see the value of that miserable situation that set me on the path to my present position. I feel good about myself for taking personal responsibility and for finding reasons to be grateful even when it was such a stretch to do so.

Viewing Our Lives in a Rear View Mirror

There's a marvelous statement made by the French novelist Collette, author of *Gigi,* the story that became a hit musical on stage and in film. "What a wonderful life I've had," she said. "I only wish I realized it sooner." Gratitude helps us enjoy each step in the journey rather than only seeing the good in retrospect.

One person who looks like he's really enjoying a wonderful life is the brilliant, multi-talented comedian Steven Colbert—new host of *The Late Show* on CBS. However, when Colbert was 10 years old, his father and two older brothers were killed in a plane crash.

During an interview with writer/editor Joel Lovell for the August 2015 issue of *GQ,* Colbert scribbled on a piece of paper: "It's our choice, whether to hate something in our lives or to love every moment of them, even the parts that bring us pain. At every moment, we are volunteers."

Rev. Dr. Michael Beckwith, founder/director of the Agape International Spiritual Center, goes so far as to say—no matter what takes place, "Call it all good!" Of course, we cannot see the good that will emerge from some calamity at the moment it occurs or even, perhaps, for years after. But in hindsight, the blessing does become visible.

When we have the perspective afforded by that long backward glance, we can see how the pieces of our life all fit together. What once may have seemed like an enormous loss or deprivation now is recognized as protection. Or perhaps it is seen as a steppingstone toward something of great value that we treasure in our life and/or that contributes profoundly to the well being of our community.

The amazing true story that became the film, *Lorenzo's Oil,* describes how Lorenzo Odone's desperate parents refused to accept the death sentence of their son's degenerative disease—and the inability of the medical community to do anything at all about it. Though completely untrained, they discovered a treatment through their relentless research that has since saved many lives around the world. With their unflagging devotion to their son, they ended up advancing medical science.

Similarly, MADD—Mother's Against Drunk Driving— has significantly cut drunk driving and alcohol-related deaths throughout the United States. The organization was founded in 1980 by Candace Lightner, following the death of her 13-year old daughter, Cari, who was struck by an intoxicated hit-and-run driver.

In the early 1990s, a writer friend of mine met and interviewed a man who'd spent 17 years in prison—mostly in solitary on death row—for a murder he did not commit. My friend asked him, "How were you able to reconcile yourself to the nightmare of being a peaceful man unjustly locked into a violent environment?" He responded, "You can't make it personal. Asking, 'Why me?' means you are taking life for granted. Why are all those children dying of starvation? I was a sacrifice. The incarceration was something that materialized. If I bailed, I couldn't contribute. What I am able to contribute is as a result of that sacrifice."

Cari was an unwanted and non-requested sacrifice, too—as was Lorenzo. The loss of their precious lives resulted in many other lives being saved. On the personal level, it might not make sense. But as the innocent and now exonerated prisoner said, "You can't make it personal." There is no question that "things happen." Our choice is to see the "lack" it creates or look for the possibilities from within the struggle. In every struggle is the opportunity to build strength.

While hardships can break us, they can also call forth from deep within us an unbreakable quality of endurance, wisdom, and compassion that might not have emerged by any other means. And who knows when we might have need for such powerful resources?

Abraham Lincoln is a classic example of perseverance in the face of persistent loss. His mother died when he was 10, his fiancée died during their engagement—leading to his nervous breakdown; he lost two sons, two businesses, and eight elections before winning the crucial election that led many to freedom from the horrors of slavery.

Based on his experiences, Lincoln concluded, "Most folks are as happy as they make up their minds to be." One of the ways we make up our minds is to live with a sense of gratitude.

Self-Real-Eyes-ation

If we were to truly and deeply "appreciate" who we are—we would not wish to be anyone else. And we would feel grateful for the particular set of challenges we were facing—not because it's the "hell we know" vs. the Heaven (or Hell) we believe that somebody else may be living. But because with the eyes of appreciation we would see how perfectly well designed our challenges are to bring out the best in us.

Scanning our life with the eyes of appreciation is like beholding a room filled with exercise equipment. We recognize it as perfectly designed to enable us to develop a strong physique—while producing endorphins in our brain and a greater sense of self-mastery. However, through the eyes of ignorance, this same exercise room in a fitness club could very well look like a torture chamber. And from any perspective, it could feel that way at times.

So we may resist going to the gym—or facing our current set of hardships— but then feel totally triumphant when we do so. With awareness, we appreciate how invaluable this set of difficulties is or was to our optimal personal development.

In her earlier years, someone I know used to say about her own life, 'It's a good thing I didn't know what was coming because I'd never have had the courage to live it." She was later privileged to meet a wheelchair bound woman who'd lost a leg and two of her beloved children. Yet, this seemingly beleaguered woman had a glorious sense of appreciation for life. Here's what this woman told her:

"All our seeming tragedies are teachers. And everybody involved in them, if they look to the higher quality of life, will see the glory in them. It's nice because life is full of glory. It's just a revolutionary process we're going through. And there's nothing tragic about it. There are circumstances beyond our control. But with that we have to give up control and see the glory, teaching, wonder and fascination of what goes on."

By training ourselves to appreciate that something much bigger is going on—as we go through the impossibly tight squeeze of incredibly painful losses and completely overwhelming challenges—we may get through these times with an incredibly rewarding sense of appreciation that "weather-proofs" us for all occasions.

Let me be clear that I am not advocating a "nobility" in suffering or poverty. Yet struggles and difficulties are built into all lives. We all have times of struggle. We will all have times of illness. Many of us will have times where we do not have as much as we need or desire. And yet, in all of those times, there are opportunities of growth and capacities for gratitude. But only when we look with eyes that see.

Thanks for Everything!

When we make a commitment to live with a grateful heart—and to share our appreciation with others—we strengthen our relationship with them. Instead of focusing on our need for other people, we give to them from the fullness of our thankful hearts. And that goes a long way to satisfying our needs from the inside out.

I once coached a man with a wonderful wife whom he dearly loved. But rather than appreciating his good fortune at having met and married such a gifted, beautiful, and supportive woman—he found himself always looking for faults in her and for reasons to be discontented. It was his negative focus—not his life situation—that created misery for him. It also created a lot of unnecessary turmoil and suffering for them both.

When I work with couples on the verge of divorce, one of the practices I recommend to them is the cultivation of gratitude and the sharing of appreciation. I ask them to view each other with different eyes, appreciative eyes. These are eyes that notice, not take for granted, all of the positive traits of a spouse.

But I'm not suggesting that they focus only on appreciating each other. I counsel them to focus on all the positive things in their lives, in general, for which they are grateful.

It really is a process of opening up one's eyes and heart to seeing and appreciating the beauty and blessings all around us. As that becomes a routine for us, we routinely live with greater gratitude and happiness.

What also happens, of course, is that we start to see everything in a more positive light—including our spouse. We see our relationships and circumstances from a more empowered and appreciative place—a place of greater fullness rather than scarcity.

By accepting and appreciating what we have, we experience peace, contentment, and a greater receptivity to our greater good. Without gratitude, we can miss the many amazing moments in our lives that may otherwise only come into focus in retrospect—when we're looking back on the photo album.

Try training your gaze on what *is* working for you rather than only on areas of displeasure. Then the conversation changes from, "You didn't give me what I wanted" to "I'm so thankful for what we have together."

Grateful No Matter What!

The ups and downs of life, the ebbs and flows, can lift us up in exaltation one moment and bring us crashing down in the next. Gratitude comes naturally when we're on top, while panic and misery are automatic responses when we feel like we can't keep going. But whether we're on the top of our game or feeling all played out, we know one thing for sure: This, too, shall pass. That's the nature of life. It is in a constant state of change.

To thrive under all conditions—instead of feeling jerked around by circumstances like a puppet controlled by strings—we have to learn to ride the waves of change while remaining upright. And one of the paramount moves in a Thriver's repertoire—as I've been endeavoring to convey in this chapter—is Thankfulness. By building this mental muscle in good times and tough times, Thrivers manage to stay strong no matter how great the challenge.

My father was a minister and there were definitely times of financial struggle when I was growing up. My folks must have felt the pressure but they never really let on. I remember conversations around the kitchen table when my father would talk about how grateful he was that there was enough—enough to pay the bills and do what was needed. We always lived with a sense of abundance and gratitude—in large part, I think, because we were a household full of love. And when love and gratitude are present, nothing is missing.

Of course, it's a whole lot easier to feel rich in love when loving people surround you. And not everybody is that lucky. But love is a quality we can amplify in our own hearts—in the midst of our family or alone on an island—by spending some concerted time savoring the grace of gratitude and seeing how we can be a blessing in other people's lives. It's an inner exercise that stimulates the production of happy hormones and beneficial neurochemicals.

Developing a Grateful Heart

Because gratefulness creates a sense of "great fullness" within us, it often puts us in a place of desiring to share from the overflow. This gratitude enhances our sense of connection with others along with the natural desire to be of service to them.

Fortunately, the attitude of gratitude is very easy to nurture. A quick and easy way to do so is by starting a Gratitude Journal in which you write down three to five things you're grateful for when you awake in the morning—and/or retire for the evening.

Writing in a Gratitude Journal is a very helpful way to start and end each day. It doesn't have to take more than five minutes or so. But like doing your morning stretches, it can improve how you feel for the rest of the day and can impact your dreams at night.

Start with the obvious blessings—feelings of gratitude for your family, your health, your intelligence, whoever and whatever is nearest and dearest to your heart. At the end of the day, focus on your wins—what went right for you that day even if what went wrong seems bigger and more compelling.

As you shift your focus to the positive, those good feelings have the chance to grow bigger within you. You will also become more attentive to the little 'wins' as they occur during the day; and your present-moment appreciation can cause them to occur more often.

Of course, there are times when we're under extra pressure, or we awaken in the morning from a troubling dream—or with a "hangover" from an unresolved argument with someone close to us the night before. Then, it's especially easy to let the negative thoughts and feelings linger in our mind and carry over into our day.

One of the strategies I use when this occurs—even before trying to switch to the "gratitude channel"—is to take a few moments to extend compassion to the place inside that feels the pain and sadness. In my experience, just by acknowledging the painful issues and feelings, they start to diminish in intensity.

Then once I feel a bit more balanced inside, I can more readily survey my life for what *is* working and what *does* feel good right now. I take a few moments to let myself breathe and savor the sweet, grateful feelings so that they can spread throughout my body. What a difference that can make to a day.

Mindfulness on the Move
If you don't have the time for this degree of self-nurturance—and your mind is racing as you jump (or drag) out of bed and fly into action—do your best to

think about some things you can feel grateful for while you're on the run and throughout your day. It becomes like a mindfulness meditation.

Tune in to your thoughts and feelings periodically while you do what needs to be done. And when you catch yourself "going over to the dark side," keep bringing your mind back to a sense of appreciation. Remember, "A thought is just a thought." You can choose whether to pursue the thoughts of "lack," or entertain the thoughts of "gratitude." Then, if there is something that needs to be done to alter the situation, you can do so from a place of clarity rather than reactivity.

Since our brain was built in a world of danger and lack, it is no surprise that it would keep dropping to that level. Those thoughts can feel all-too-real, even though they are just creations of the mind. Of course, our minds create the higher thoughts, too. We are just in the habit of believing and listening to those lower, less helpful, thoughts.

You can reinforce your commitment to make this shift in perspective by regularly writing in your gratitude journal when time allows. It also helps to read these entries whenever you need a reminder that better times are behind you *and* ahead.

Some days this can feel like a strenuous mental workout. But if you practice a bit each day, it starts to become habitual and automatic. Your mind begins looking for things to feel good about instead of looking to "pick-a-bone" with someone about something—or nothing at all.

Sharing Our Gratitude: Appreciation

We all tend to spend so much of our time walking around concerned with what we don't have, what we can't do, what's not in our life. But if we keep a gratitude journal we are consciously choosing a different view. We're looking for the things for which we are grateful. And it really does affect our mood and physiology.

I like to find as many ways as possible to boost the dopamine in my brain. One of the ways I do this is by expressing my appreciation to others—even strangers. It brightens their day, which also makes my heart happy.

There are lots of ways to do this—a tweet, a text, an email, a phone call, a Facebook post, or a post card in the mail. There are so many easy and convenient ways to share appreciation with others. And who knows how far the good feelings generated by that simple gesture might travel from person-to-person?

Make a practice of feeling grateful and expressing appreciation every day for at least 30 days. The positive effects on your mood will also create long-term benefits for your brain and reset how it operates so that a more positive disposition becomes the default setting.

Gratitude is the internal sense of thankfulness. Appreciation is the point when we share it. As William Arthur Ward stated, "Feeling gratitude and not expressing it is like wrapping a present and not giving it."

Balancing Life's Ledger Sheet

Even though we know we're not supposed to—when we're feeling in low spirits it can seem so much more "natural" to count our neighbor's blessings rather than our own. It can, in fact, feel like a compulsion.

The problem with this, of course, is that it puts us on a downward spiral of insatiable wanting, longing, and hankering after—which, like a tornado, can quickly gather velocity and strip the meaning and value from our lives (at least in our own estimation). No matter who we are, what we have and how much we may have overcome to be where we are today—all we can see in such moments is failure.

Millionaires with large yachts have been known to feel inadequate next to billionaires with even larger ones. So no one is immune to this self-destructive tendency. And there really is no limit to how big this snowball can grow as it tumbles directly to hell.

The 17th Century poet, John Milton wrote in his epic work, *Paradise Lost,* "The mind is its own place, and in itself can make a heaven of hell, a hell of heaven." Climbing the ladder out of hell and into the heaven of gratitude and acceptance can take enormous strength at first. But it's the kind of strength we can build over time—step-by-step—by developing the daily gratitude habit.

Making a practice of focusing on the positive side of the ledger of life, and building a mental muscle by expressing our appreciation every day—for even the smallest of blessings—can create an upward spiral of elevating energies that lifts our spirits above our issues, enabling us to walk through life feeling wealthy beyond measure regardless of what's in our bank account.

Both of these practices are simple to do—but just as easy not to do. We simply have to catch ourselves early in the process to make sure we're going in the direction we desire because the momentum builds up so quickly.

Of course, there are times when we just take a "time out" to feel sorry for ourselves. And that's perfectly okay, and completely understandable. We just need to do so with conscious intention so we don't get swept away on a torrent of tears. Minds do what minds have done habitually. Those habits do return. No need to create yet another point of self-recrimination. Just reset your intention, allow the thought to drop, and move forward.

Yes, it's a strenuous work out at times. But the interest you take and investment you make in your own mental hygiene is compounded daily. And the dividends it pays throughout your life grow in value and abundance.

What We're Really Hankering For

It can help to understand the secret behind the illusion of "less than …". So, here's what I think we really are after when we feel shortchanged in relation to others. In my view, it isn't really greater attributes or opportunities, relationships and possessions that we're longing for to "even the score"—though it can certainly seem that way. But what we're lacking and needing first and foremost is a greater **appreciation** of who and what we already are—but in a different sense of that very rich word.

If you go on-line to dictionary.com you'll see that "Appreciation"—in addition to being so closely related to gratitude, and to an increase in value (when it comes to money)—also means this, among other things:

- *Thankful* recognition of value
- The act of *estimating the qualities of things and giving them their proper value*; and
- *Clear perception or recognition*, especially of aesthetic quality

What could be of greater value to us than an appreciation of our true value in our own eyes? The more we appreciate ourselves—in the broader senses of this world—the less we feel *less than* the people around us. And the more we learn to appreciate our deeper beauty, inner value, and often-overlooked good fortune, the happier we are with our lives. Then, we have a tendency to attract and notice more positive experiences.

Unearthing Buried Treasure

Discovering how profoundly amazing we are can take a lifetime, because we underestimate our capabilities. We have far greater capacities than we realize, as young children and late bloomers both frequently demonstrate. And as long as we live with a learning orientation toward life, there will always be new traits to discover and new trails to pursue.

Of course, there's another big reason why it can take a whole lifetime to fully appreciate just how magnificent we naturally are. If we grew up with a bad case of the "not-enuff-stuff"—as so many of us did, due to misguided parenting (from parents who grew up the same way) and negative cultural programming—it's easy to split-off from inner aspects and talents that authority figures deemed worthless and unacceptable.

Who knows what hidden resources got buried along with these disowned aspects? And how can we feel whole and complete if we jettisoned important, unexplored parts along the way? It can be very hard to appreciate—in all senses of that word—our true value as a unique human being, if it wasn't reflected back to us continuously since we were very young.

So, in addition to writing in your gratitude journal about what you appreciate in your life, how about adding each day an expression of gratitude for something you're learning to appreciate about yourself? With just one of these daily self-loving "supplements," you'll grow a whole new sense of appreciation for yourself in the course of a few weeks or months.

The Transforming Power of Gratitude

There is more than one kind of gratitude. We're all familiar with the perfunctory kind in which we go through the motions but don't experience the emotion.

Then there is the actual energetic experience of Gratitude where we move into the feeling of great fullness, which induces a sense of awe, humility and the presence of the sacred in our everyday life. We feel how blessed and cared for we actually are.

Like beholding a magnificent sunset that takes our breath away, we feel nurtured and embraced with love by life, itself. Having that kind of experience on a regular basis is what changes our neurochemistry and neural networks. That's the real power of gratitude.

We began this book talking about paradigms and the lens through which we view the world. Filling our hearts with gratefulness helps us to see "through a glass clearly" and respond appropriately through the eyes of love.

What if you can actually become a bigger person, simply by nurturing one habit? Can you picture yourself going through life with gratitude in your heart instead of the feeling of a great hole in your soul that you desperately try to fill up with "stuff?" That's something that you—and only you—can actually give to yourself. And when you do so you become such a beautiful energetic presence wherever you go.

Post Script on Gratitude

When we really invest in cultivating the energy of gratitude, something remarkable can happen. It can take on a life of its own. And, in unexpected moments, the sensation of Gratitude can descend upon us like a mantle of Grace that stirs the heart, slows the mind, and calms the spirit with a sense of total trust and peacefulness.

When such moments come to pass, give them time and space so you can breathe them in and let them fill you up. If you can, just close your eyes and sit quietly in this. Let gratitude grow and expand within you.

If you haven't had this experience yet, know that it awaits you. And no doubt you've met its closest "cousin," which is the feeling of tremendous relief that comes over us when all the fear and tension we didn't even know we were carrying suddenly drains away and we see clearly again.

TL;DR—Practice Gratitude

- Gratitude is a practice. It is not a result of having everything, but a result of nurturing a sense of gratitude for what you do have.

- The switch from striving to thriving is the switch from wanting to gratitude. In a culture that is driven by using insecurity to fuel consumerism, gratitude is a realization that everything is a gift.

- Gratitude is not about settling for what you have, but recognizing that what you have can be held gratefully.

- Gratitude is a practice, a discipline. Because our primitive mind is built on wanting and needing, we have to make a shift to our higher brain. That requires some effort, until it is the new habit.

- Use a Gratitude Journal to build a gratitude mindset and habit. A Gratitude Journal is simply a method of writing several things for which you are thankful (unique each day), and then reflecting on those items at the other side of the day. You can record those items in the morning or evening, and then reflect upon them and hold the feeling of gratitude in your awareness in the evening or morning. This creates a habit, and also creates a new outlook, of looking for that for which you are grateful.

- Appreciation is the outward expression of Gratitude. While gratitude is the feeling you may hold, when you share that feeling with the person connected, it is Appreciation. This builds your own gratitude mindset and the positive regard in the relationship.

Chapter 8

practice everyday spirituality

"There are two ways to live. You can live as if nothing is a miracle, or you can live as if everything is a miracle."
—Albert Einstein

ncreasing numbers of people are describing themselves as spiritual, rather than religious. So what's the difference? Here's how I see it.

A religion is a particular set of beliefs and practices for worshipping whatever someone means when they use the word "God" (or "gods.") These beliefs and practices may include precepts for how best to live life and what to expect after life is over. Someone who subscribes to these beliefs can be described as "religious."

In fact, the root of the word, "religion" is "relegio," which means "to regulate." It is based in regulating belief and function within a particular institution (church or other faith institution).

Within a religious denomination, there are variations in beliefs and practices that lead those who adhere to them to cluster together into a subset or sect of that particular denomination. And for some strange reason, conviction in the correctness of a particular religion's or sect's beliefs about the unknowable have led to incredible, sometimes violent disagreements that contradict that religion's original message of peace and loving kindness to all.

In my view, while religion is a set of ideas and practices of a faith group, spirituality focuses on deeper internal experiences that unite people of all backgrounds in a compassionate respect for our shared humanity and all creation.

This is not to take away from any specific religious belief system. I do not mean to criticize or downgrade any faith tradition. Only to say that "religion" and "spirituality" are two different elements of belief systems that are often confused. Being "deeply religious" and "deeply spiritual" are two different metrics, not to be confused.

So what would qualify as a genuinely spiritual experience? I would say that anything that helps us to more deeply connect with our inner life—leading to a greater sense of connection with all of life. When one has such an experience, it can cause us to reformulate our views about the nature of reality, our particular place within it, and the purpose of our lives. It resets our relationship with all of creation.

Of course, people can be both religious and spiritual. But it's also possible to be religious yet not have an awakened sense of the spiritual within us. We can just be "going along with the program," but not really feeling whether it matches our own worldview and life experience. On the other hand, one can be deeply spiritual, yet claim no formal religion at all.

A World Where Miracles Abound

For young children full of wonder and curiosity, Earth can seem like Wonderland. What happens as we get older is that we stop wondering and assume we already "know." In fact, the more sophisticated and "worldly" we become, the more mundane the world may appear to us to be. Nothing has actually changed, of course, except the lens through which we view it.

We've all had dreams while sleeping in which the weird and improbable seems completely commonplace. It isn't until we awaken and remember a glimmer of our dream that we realize how totally weird the images were that we were accepting while we were dreaming as totally normal. Once someone "awakens," in the spiritual sense, the person becomes aware of the inter-connectedness of all of us. One becomes aware of the wonder of being in the world, and of the world even being in the vast Cosmos. One becomes more aware and connected to the Sacred.

Just think about the improbability of your own existence—in this moment of time in this unbelievably vast universe. Ponder for a second how many of your ancestors—from the beginning of human life—had to get together at just the right time and place for you to be who, what, and where you are right now. A staggering number of "chance" encounters—which could have as easily not happened—had to occur for you to be you, here, now. Is this anything short of miraculous?

We're accustomed to thinking of miracles as something out of the ordinary—and yet what we call "ordinary" is, itself, miraculous. It's just that we've gotten so accustomed to seeing it that we've mostly stopped seeing it for what it is.

Think for a moment about a tree: It is made of a substance we call "wood" that emerges from a tiny seed in the dirt. This tiny seed contains a very complicated and detailed set of instructions that turns it into a powerful processing plant with the capacity to convert sunlight, water, and minerals into everything required for it to grow for centuries into a towering structure that can feed, house, and provide warmth and shelter for many life forms. From a negligible seed—carried by the wind or dropped by a bird—it has grown into an essential and indivisible component of a vast eco-system.

Even when the tree dies and is ultimately reduced to dust, it will still serve the greater community of life. Doesn't that sound incredibly miraculous to you—and more bizarre than any dream you've ever had?

Miracles surround and indwell us. You may have no detailed knowledge of how your food is digested, your blood is circulated, or your children came into being (other than the fun part). Part of the miracle is that we don't have to understand these complicated processes for them to work perfectly well for us. The requisite knowledge is already programmed into the cells of our body, which carry out all the tasks and operations required for us to live healthy lives.

Life, itself, is the greatest of all miracles. And all we have to do is to open our eyes and hearts to perceive it. It's when we do that that we have what I would call a spiritual experience. As Michael Beckwith describes it, "You cease taking for granted things that on the surface appear to be part and parcel of life: friendship, love, community, home, birds, music, flowers, sunshine. Gratitude informs your heart and heightens your awareness of the underlying Presence in these soulful experiences."

Some people believe that thriving has nothing to do with appreciation for what we might call "ordinary miracles." But being able to appreciate the incredible miracle of our every moment on this tiny planet imbues us with such feelings of gratitude, awe, humility, and unity that we cannot help but be in a thriving mindset. And this mindset is what I would call "everyday spirituality."

As earlier mentioned, a friend of mine met a man in her church who had recently been released from prison after serving years on death row for a murder he did not commit. When she later asked him how he enjoyed the service he shook his head and said, "I saw all of these people rushing to church, stepping on flowers."

Truly, there is so much beauty around us all the time yet we rarely stop to notice, appreciate, and revel in it. We're usually so caught up in our perpetual cycles of needing and wanting and having and wasting, which can only lead us in endless circles of suffering. When we step out of the circle to "smell the roses" and appreciate their beauty, we refresh ourselves with a sense of the sacred that can alter our experience of the moment.

What Do Spiritual People Believe?

While religions can divide—often creating an "Us against Them" mentality—spirituality nurtures our sense of connectedness. As we cultivate our spirituality, we feel more deeply and consciously connected to our own greater Self, to every other being, to the unfathomable mystery of life, the exquisite beauty of nature, and the unimaginable vastness of the universe.

Thrivers consciously nurture their spirituality. They don't wait for something outside themselves to trigger a heightened experience of connection with the All. And they don't wait until they are stressed out to seek and find that inner place of peace. They go about making a space for the sacred every day in their hearts, their minds, and their lives.

People may argue about whether or not there is a God (or what God is like). But, there really is no arguing about a spiritual experience because often, there aren't even any words to describe it. It's a palpable state of involuntary appreciation and awe that causes our hearts to expand and our heads to bow as we behold the miracle of this existence.

Spirituality is a natural, inherent component of life that people experience each in their own way. Over the last several decades, a wide variety of spiritual teachers, practices, and communities have emerged. Most share basic assumptions, even if they teach a very different approach for actualizing them in life. Here's how I would sum up these assumptions:

- The Source of all Creation exists everywhere in creation, permeating the world, seen and unseen, within and without.
- All human beings have a capacity to experience a connection with this Source. There may simply be those who are more aware of it than others and who actively seek to expand their awareness.
- Each of us has direct access to our own spirituality and to the greater wisdom within ourselves.
- We are all creators—with our thoughts, beliefs, words, and the focus of our attention, as well as through our actions.
- The more we focus on the indwelling beauty in ourselves and other people, the more it grows within us.
- The potential to do great good in the world—as well as great evil—is within each of us.
- Life is all about guiding our journey with the "rudder" of intention, and moving in the direction of our dreams and beliefs, moment-by-moment, choice-by-choice.

The more we choose to nurture our awareness of the spiritual in the everyday, the more resilient and compassionate we become. One common trait of spirituality from the East and West is the awareness of connection to other people and to the greater world. When we experience what has been called "unity consciousness," we know our acts of kindness toward others actually nurture our own hearts and bring peace to our own minds—as well as benefitting others.

Heartfelt generosity and kindness come from a place within that is bigger than our little self—with all its hungers, bothers, and complaints. When we are in that generous space in our own consciousness, we are living with an expanded sense of our inherent belonging to the whole interconnected web of life. And what a powerfully nourishing experience that is!

Practicing Human Kindness

One of my friends has a great knack for meeting people. For her, a stranger is just friend she hasn't made yet. So, she's not shy about talking to people in an elevator, while waiting for an airplane, in a grocery store, or wherever people congregate. This is especially true if she senses a kindred spirit or sees someone in need of a friendly smile or a helping hand.

When she was growing up, this woman never felt seen or validated by her family. She is thus painfully aware of how important it is to be recognized as a person of value. So that's what she endeavors to communicate when she smiles wholeheartedly at another person and looks directly into their eyes. She knows this may be her one and only encounter with that person. So, she seeks to impart a gift of recognition that they can take to heart and then share with others. By seeking to touch the heart of another with love, she heals her own heart.

Years ago, I read of a counselor who received a note from a formerly incarcerated youth who had gone on to achieve great things in his life. The note was full of appreciation for this counselor's powerful influence in helping him turn his whole life around. But the counselor had no recollection of him at all.

When the counselor had the opportunity to meet the man who sent the note, he asked to be reminded of their prior interactions. The man told him that they'd only met once before. But on that occasion the counselor had told him how bright he was and what potential he had to succeed in his life. It was the first time he'd ever heard such words of praise directed to him. And it changed the whole course of his life.

The counselor's comments and the woman's smiles are expressions of everyday spirituality. And we have no idea the impact such simple acts may have on other people's lives and on the wider world.

Both the woman and the counselor had intentions. They both sought to bring more love and connection into the world. They had no way of knowing all the ways their actions have impacted others. When you decide to become more intentional about showing care and expressing love in the world, you must simply trust the ripples this creates. You may only see the impact here and there. But as that joins with others doing the same, the impact grows. And as the woman tells me, magic tends to happen when we're living with such intentions.

Less Than Perfect

The Tibetan Buddhist nun, Pema Chodron, talks about something else that can happen when we cultivate our everyday spirituality by watching our mind as part of a meditative practice: We may quickly discover that we're really not such a nice person after all. The sorts of weaknesses and flaws we've noticed and condemned in other people turn out to be fully present in our own minds. When we tune in to the incessant chatter, we sometimes hear the voice of jealousy, complaint, nastiness, pettiness, judgment—and all those other thoughts and tendencies we may not have previously acknowledged in ourselves.

The miracle is that once we understand more fully just how far short of perfect all of us fall, we tend to be a lot more forgiving of ourselves and other people. After all, we are truly "only human." And the human "mind"—like computers—comes with some common "bugs" that we have to be aware of and compensate for in order to be at our best as much of the time as humanly possible.

As we already discussed, the "fight, flight, or freeze" reaction pattern of our survival system evolved to protect us in an environment that couldn't be more different than the one we live in today. So we have to implement certain "manual fixes" to keep us sane and balanced in a world that's both far less and far more stressful than our ancient ancestors ever experienced. We also have to exercise restraint and discretion when it comes to putting our thoughts into action.

Watching our mind makes it possible to see the unlovely tendencies that some people act on automatically. We can watch a feeling arise, such as jealousy, note the thought that is causing that feeling, recognize it as simply a thought, breathe through the sensation without reaction or judgment, and then watch it dissipate.

Watching the mind also awakens us to our unconscious beliefs and assumptions. One of my friends discovered that while he endeavored to be kind to everyone he encountered, once he was behind the wheel of his car, he suddenly felt he had the license to pursue his own agenda. He thought nothing of edging in front of others, zipping around cars, and honking when someone "did unto him" precisely what he was doing unto everyone else.

It's amazing how long it can take us to notice the obvious contradictions in our own behavior. But as Arthur Conan Doyle's famous character, Sherlock Holmes pointed out, "The world is full of obvious things which nobody by any chance ever observes."

We are, perhaps, most oblivious to our own foibles. When we have an "awakening experience," we may suddenly notice the obvious contradictions between our "Talk" and our "Walk." Once we do so, then other people's foibles don't seem as egregious to us after all. And we can bring our behavior into alignment with our beliefs.

A softer, kinder heart not only makes forgiveness a whole lot easier, it also brings gratitude to the forefront of our awareness. And as we see beyond our own noses, we recognize that miracles abound all around us. We see, as well, that true wonder, joy, and fulfillment can mainly be found within our own hearts, in our relationships with others, and in the world around us.

The Peace That Surpasses . . .

Another of the many advantages of cultivating one's natural spirituality is that it calms the mind. Remember all that background noise from the constant mental chatter? On and on it goes with, "I need this; I want that; I must have this; I hate that; who does she think she is . . . ." It's so often about scarcity, judgment, and complaint. And that's an awful place to have to spend our lives.

The mind is running all the time—a ceaseless stream of predominantly meaningless babble. That's just what a mind does. And when things are not going well for us, it's easy for the thoughts to get particularly muddy and unpleasant. Staying tuned-in and aware of the content of our thoughts—so we can choose which ones to listen to and which to ignore—is both a spiritual practice and a strategy for thriving.

When the mind calms down as we breathe into the present moment, we start to feel the "enoughness" of who we are, how we are, and what we have. The constant pull, rush, and pressure of the survival mind working overtime to protect us from perceived (but often false) threats—finally gets to relax and give way to the growing warmth and peace of our own sense of okay-ness.

One of the common traits of people who thrive is that they know that they are going to be okay in the long run, regardless of what's happening now. They may feel the pain and chaos of the moment. But ultimately, they know that everything will get sorted out and they'll move on from there.

Of course, at times when we've suffered an enormous loss, we can feel completely overwhelmed and hopeless. We are amazed that the sun still rises and sets the following day. We wonder how things could go on as usual when everything for us has changed forever.

And yet, it does. Life gets back on-track. Grief finds gratitude (you don't grieve what you don't miss, and what you miss is worthy of gratitude). Life moves forward, and you with it.

Regularly cultivating our spiritual nature gives us greater patience to endure whatever challenges life brings our way. It also endows us with a long-term perspective on life that helps us abide when it ebbs and flourish when it flows. Everyday spirituality calms the mind as we shift our focus away from fear, scarcity, pain or loss to the peace and clarity within us and beyond everything else.

Spirituality Rearranges Our Priorities

How many times do we find ourselves so wrapped up in petty arguments, disagreements, and frustrations—that what started out as a small thing gets blown out of all proportion? Such "much ado about nothing" has wrecked many a life and relationship.

What happens to many people at the end of their life is that this all becomes clear. On the edge of life and death it's like the fog finally lifts and we see the sun, the moon, and the stars as if for the very first time.

Now nothing matters so much as our loving connections with the people who are near and dear to us. And that's the real legacy we leave behind. It resides in the hearts of everyone we've touched, all the relationships we've nurtured, all the people whose lives we've helped to improve—including those strangers we only met once along the way.

Too many people wait until the very last moment to learn this essential truth. One of the many blessings we create for ourselves through a spiritual practice is an ever-expanding awareness of what's really important in life. We discover that relationships with others—our connections in the world—are really what is most important.

When we keep this in the forefront of our awareness, which is what happens when we cultivate a spiritual consciousness, we endeavor to put our loving into action. We discover that a loving spirit pulls us outward and brings us pleasure while a grasping mind creates a painful inner contraction.

As long as we maintain our sense of separation from Life—from the world of other people and our own deeper sense of Self—we get trapped in feelings of inadequacy. We feel short-changed by life, cheated by others, left out in the cold, or left behind. That's when it can be helpful to read the perspective of someone for whom such a hellish experience was once profoundly real.

Dr. Viktor Frankl lost his entire family in the Holocaust. In order to survive, he had to find a way to create a meaningful life for himself amidst the constant brutality and senseless daily mass murders. He found that meaning by serving his fellow inmates. One of the things he observed in his book, *Man's Search for Meaning,* is that, "People have enough to live by but nothing to live for; they have the means but no meaning."

Nurturing our innate spirituality—with all that it leads us to feel, to discover, to share, and to do—is a very important way we can give our life more meaning every day. All we have to do is to take a little time every day to discover our greater Self more fully.

Eight Steps to Greater Inner Freedom

Thrivers don't wait for something outside themselves—or some special moment—to randomly generate a peak experience or a sense of the sacred. We can do this for ourselves any time we find a sacred time and place in which to experience it.

Given how many spiritual paths and practices there are, I want to share with you just eight simple practices that I've found especially helpful over the years. You might want to use these as a general guideline while you seek to discover what works best for you.

If you find that a practice helps you open your heart and deepens your appreciation of life, you're definitely on the right tract. And if you stick with it, you'll be amazed at how you grow and thrive over time.

We've already discussed many of the practices I'll briefly describe here that nurture our spiritual nature. Any and all of these strategies—if regularly utilized—can enhance our awareness of our innate beauty of being.

1. **Focus on Peak Experiences**: The first spiritual practice that I am suggesting involves sitting quietly for a little while—perhaps upon arising and/ or before retiring for the day. It could also be at any time during the day when you need a "time out" from the rush of pressures and activities and a "tune-up" for whatever is next in your day.

While you sit, conjure in your memory a peak experience. Then, let yourself recall it with all your senses as fully engaged as possible. Experiences of this nature are well named because we're essentially given a moment of clarity in which we get to peek into something truly extraordinary that takes our breath away.

We've all had these kinds of experiences at least once in our lives and probably more than that. So think back upon a moment that caught you by surprise. Perhaps it was in childhood, seeing snow or the ocean for the very first time. Or maybe you were awe-struck when you peered over the edge of the Grand Canyon and your mind went silent.

For many, these moments come at the end of an exertion: Pulling yourself to the top of a rock wall, hiking to the bottom of a gorge, running a marathon and crossing the tape. Or even completing a creative or mental exertion—such as finishing that book, working on that painting, or pulling that beautiful ceramic from the kiln.

How about when you held your newborn child in your arms and felt a quality of awe, wonder, and love that you never even knew existed? Can you recall what that was like and feel it again in your heart? Close your eyes, deepen your breath, and let the feelings rise in you and spread throughout your body. Then, remain in that space for as long as you possibly can. When you come out of it, notice how you're feeling and what you are experiencing.

Maybe it's some surpassing work of art that lifts you above the mundane and gives you a peak experience. Or maybe it's an epiphany you had in which the secret behind some mystery was suddenly revealed to you. Recall how you were taken aback or startled into silence and sudden contemplation as you wondered about the wonder of it all.

These sorts of experiences give us a taste of the sacred, which is ever-present in the midst of the ordinary. They also help us see ourselves, our lives, and the whole world within a much larger context.

I know for myself, that running through the woods or paddling on a wood-lined river, connects me to the natural world and to the beauty that surrounds me. It catapults me into my heart—and simultaneously to the heart of all that exists, and awakens me more fully to my connection with all Creation. I get that same awe from paddling on the water and staring at the expanse of ocean, the water undulating in waves from across the sea. The water almost seems to come alive in the waves and currents.

Peak experiences can also occur when we are being of service in the world. The opportunity to show up in someone else's life—perhaps a stranger—at just the right moment to fill an urgent need can set waves of gratitude moving through our body. We may even feel as if we'd been somehow guided to be the "right person at the right place and time" to make a lasting, positive difference for another individual. This, in turn, can heighten our sense of being an integral, valuable part of a greater Reality than we normally notice in our daily life.

Peak experiences generate a heightened state of aliveness, and fill us with awe and gratitude. They're rarely about getting more "stuff"—though that can certainly feel exciting in the moment. But peak experiences are often beyond excitement. In fact, they may produce a deeper sense of calm and quiet within us as we sense the invisible web of existence gently holding us in its embrace.

Peak experiences include anything that precipitates a spontaneous up-welling of love that overtakes us and spills out into the world. Maybe it's the relief that comes after a lab test returns with a negative diagnosis on what had looked like a very serious illness. At that moment, your appreciation for your health, your life, and the love of your family and friends absolutely stuns you into silence. This is the kind of experience you seek to remember for yourself and then dwell on as long as possible. Afterwards, notice how you feel.

Many times, a peak experience finds us unexpectedly. We are in the midst of an activity and suddenly, the moment hits us. We are pulled into a peak experience. But we also always have a choice to recall such peak experiences, to reimagine and re-experience them, whenever we wish.

2. **Discover Sacred Space**: Have you ever entered a space in which you sensed a beautiful, palpable energy that feels calming and sacred to you? For some people, it's their meditation room. For others, it's an established place of worship like a church, mosque, or synagogue. But the energy that lingers there from people's prior inward journeys actually makes it easier to take that journey again and again.

We can directly touch the sacred when in Nature—by letting our mind focus on bird song while our thoughts drift away with the breeze. As I've already shared, for me, a strenuous run through the woods or paddling on the river takes me out of my busy mind and into a greater reality. So I do these activities as often as possible.

I also enter sacred space when I'm living my purpose by serving other people as a coach or in some other capacity. By doing what I love every day, my heart and spiritual consciousness expand. As a result, over time, I have become a much more peaceful, pleasant, happy version of myself—even when I'm dealing with a lot of stress.

You might want to make a list of some of the most special moments in your life, where they occurred, and how you felt when they happened. Then—give yourself the opportunity to enjoy such quality experiences by repeating them as often as possible. And/or take the time to put yourself back there in your memory on a regular basis and recreate the experience for yourself visually and energetically. Breathe it in, feel it—and give thanks for it. Keeping such moments alive in our hearts allows us to refresh ourselves whenever we need reminding that who and what we are is far greater than whatever stresses and challenges are going on for us in the moment.

Remember that a sacred space for one person may be hollow for another. Seek out *your* sacred space. Don't worry too much if it is your space, alone. It may be one that many share. Or it may feel sacred only to you.

3. **Practice Prayer and Meditation**: When meditation was first becoming popular in the West, some people described it as "navel gazing," as if it fostered self-preoccupation. But what actually happens for most people is that their meditation practice liberates them from the prison of the little self. In fact, the more we quiet ourselves—even if only for a few moments, the more we touch upon the universals that link us to the whole world and beyond.

That's why so many people who meditate take steps to become a beneficial presence in other people's lives. They have come to see themselves as part of a greater whole and their empathy expands to embrace a wider expanse of life. Meditators come to see that we are not really separate from each other at all. We all go through similar stresses and pains, joys and blessings in life. Knowing this, we can more readily extend our kindness toward others—with an enhanced recognition that we simultaneously do this for ourselves.

There is no one right way—or best way—to meditate and pray. You can learn various techniques and then see which ones most resonate with you and assist you in entering sacred space. But there really is no mystery to meditating. We can create techniques and approaches. In essence, you are simply heightening your awareness of your self and your mind, then learning to set that aside.

I recommend that you practice meditation at least once a day—through awareness of your breath, by quieting your mind, and perhaps by focusing on your heart—whatever method you like. By whatever means you use, seek to feel connected with the greater life within and around us all.

Such connections are what change us in beneficial ways as human beings. For instance, when we focus on our own hearts—perhaps offering compassionate understanding to the sadness or loneliness we might find there and then nurturing our hearts with our own love—they cannot help but grow, like flowers, with greater compassion.

For many, prayer serves this same purpose. It brings in an awareness of the needs of the world, our lack of control in this world, and our connection to the Divine. For me, my prayers are of gratitude. I find that when I move toward requests, I shift away from appreciation and amazement to requests for more. So, I practice saying "Thank You."

As the German theologian, mystic, and philosopher, Meister Eckhart stated, "If the only prayer you ever say in your entire life is thank you, it will be enough."

4. **Practice Mindfulness**: So much of the time we operate unconsciously and on automatic. When we practice mindfulness, we bring our whole awareness to the present moment.

If you'd like to have an experience of that right now—as you're reading these words—become aware of your surroundings and of how you're sitting or standing at the moment. What does your weight feel like in the seat or on your feet? What sounds are happening around you that you may have tuned out until this moment? Become aware of these sounds. Become aware of the sensations of your body. Whatever you're doing in this moment, focus on it fully.

If you're practicing mindful eating, savor the flavor, concentrate on the texture, the fragrance, the sensation of chewing and swallowing, and the feeling that occurs when the food moves from your mouth to your stomach. Mindfulness is not really about getting or doing anything. It's about gaining greater mastery over our mind such that we can really be present for our own experience in the moment instead of performing absent-minded multi-tasking while living in the past or future.

Our mind pulls us in so many directions toward a multitude of distractions while at the same time going "off-line." Imagine how effective we could be in our lives if we learned to *Be Here Now*—which was the name of one of the most popular early books in the human potential movement. Training the mind to stay focused by practicing mindfulness for a little while each day is like training a dog to follow our lead instead of dragging us along on a walk.

Through this practice, we mindfully remember (or learn) that a "thought is just a thought." We don't have to give it any more time, weight, or energy than that—unless, of course, there's something important that needs our attention. Our mindfulness practice can deliver us from the stuck places in our thinking by getting us out of our heads and focused on the feeling of being alive right now.

5. **Be On Purpose**: There's so little in our culture that promotes the awareness that happiness comes from using our gifts to be of service to other people. The psychiatrist Karl A. Menninger pointed out that "Love cures people—both the ones who give it and the ones who receive it." Thus, as Dr. Menninger recommended, when you're feeling in low spirits, go be compassionately helpful to someone else. It's not just about helping people and being of service in the world. It's about finding some activity that nourishes your soul and amplifies your sense of the sacred. And this often happens when we're being creative and when we're using our creative gifts in loving service to others.

6. **Practice Forgiveness**: Forgiveness is based in spirituality. It's a decision to let go of the grudge, created by negative emotions. By nurturing our innate spirituality, we find something that feels so much better and more worthwhile than holding a grudge. Thus, we more readily let go of anger and blame.

Inspirational author Catherine Ponder says that, "When you hold resentment toward another, you are bound to that person or condition by an emotional link that is stronger than steel. Forgiveness is the only way to dissolve that link and get free." Forgiveness is within your power—once you recognize that it's something you do for yourself in order to move forward without encumbrances from the past.

Embrace forgiveness as a choice you can make, regardless of the actions of anyone else. You can choose to practice forgiveness, because forgiving is always your own self-honoring choice.

7. **Practice Gratitude and Appreciation**: Gratitude is a habit to develop. As mentioned, a starting point for gratitude involves contemplating—and preferably writing down (so as to reinforce)—three, four, or five things for which you're especially grateful, each day. You can do this at any time, but it's especially helpful at the beginning and/or end of each day.

Focusing on gratitude can heighten our awareness of the miraculous in our everyday reality. This, in turn, can shift our consciousness from "half-empty" to "half-full." And when we practice gratitude regularly, our half-full cup can feel "over the top," allowing us to share the overflow with others.

Watch what happens when you express your appreciation to another person. Chances are, it may induce gratitude to flow more freely from their hearts, too. And as you share this appreciation with each other, you create sacred space together, which you can re-enter in your mind whenever you desire.

8. **Be inspired**: So many resources, from books to retreats, videos to speeches, can enrich our spiritual lives. Never before have these resources been so close to us. So much material is just a click away.

It is so much better and enriching to fill ourselves with such material rather than the negative "stuff" that also surrounds us 24 hours per day. The stress of watching the world's evils and struggles does nothing to fill our souls or build our thriving lives.

Go and find your inspiration. And remember that the word, "inspire," means to breathe in spirit. To take spirit into you is to honor and practice your spirituality.

Spirituality Every Day

Becoming a more spiritual person doesn't mean that you become a perfect person. As long as you're in a body, you're going to be imperfect. That's just how it is.

Being spiritual definitely doesn't mean that you become "holier than thou" or an all-knowing sage who purports to know what's best for other people. In fact, one hallmark of true spirituality is becoming more humble, more empathetic, and more reticent to offer unwanted advice.

Spirituality also doesn't require that you withdraw from ordinary life to live in an ashram or monastery, to devote yourself to a spiritual "master" or to adopt a way of life at great variance with your own nature and way of being. Spirituality is part of the everyday—whoever you are, wherever you are—when you become aware of and open to it. It's what helps us to experience the amazing nature of ordinary, in good moments and tough times.

If a spiritual teacher or organization does require you to withdraw from the world, my suggestion is either to run the other way or do a whole lot of research before submitting yourself to someone else's prescription for your life. Sometimes, pulling away is a good refresher, but not a great way of living a full life.

Winston Churchill once described Russia this way: "It is a riddle, wrapped in a mystery, inside an enigma." What an apt description that is for life itself.

Practicing everyday spirituality keeps us in touch with the deep mystery at the heart of our existence. It enables us to open ourselves regularly to experience the beauty, bounty, and miraculous quality of the Mystery. And as we do so, we naturally partake of these qualities by becoming more beautiful, bountiful, wise, and miraculous ourselves. In other words, we thrive.

TL;DR—Practice Everyday Spirituality

- Spirituality is not the same as religion. You can experience spirituality, regardless of your religious beliefs. And you can practice religion, but have no sense of spirituality.
- Spirituality is a connection of your deepest Self to yourself, others, and all creation. It is an awareness of the miracle of being here, along with everything else being here.
- Here are eight steps to nurture your own everyday spirituality:
  1. Focus on Peak Experiences. Many people refer to these moments as "mountaintop experiences," filled with amazement. It often comes in the midst of physical exertion, but can also come in the moments of being overwhelmed with a sense of awe. Remember those moments and focus on the feelings associated with them.
  2. Discover Sacred Space. Where you experience the Sacred may vary. Some find it in the architecture of places of worship. Others find it in nature. Still others find it in solace and meditation, wherever they are. Find your Sacred Space and make sure to visit often.
  3. Practice prayer and/or meditation. There are many types of prayer and many types of meditation. Find the methods that speak to your Self and fit within your own belief systems. Then make it a practice to practice them.
  4. Practice mindfulness. Mindfulness is bringing a full awareness into the current moment, experiencing what is happening, not the thoughts that keep us insulated from the experience. If you are eating, experience the sensations and tastes of the food. If you are walking, experience the sense of connection to the ground, to what is beneath you. If you are conversing, experience the conversation between you, not the conversation of your mind.
  5. Be on purpose. Find a place of purpose in your life that takes you outside of yourself and into a bigger reason.

6. Practice forgiveness. When we practice forgiveness, we are practicing being connected lovingly to others (and to ourselves).

7. Practice gratitude and appreciation. The spiritual is not about having more and more, but appreciating what is. It is the gratitude of being who you are, where you are, with what you have.

8. Be inspired. Find activities that breathe life and spirit into you. Seek out resources and events that nurture your inspiration. Don't leave that to chance. Find the places and events that inspire, surround yourself with people and objects which inspire.

Chapter 9

maintain boundaries

Years ago, I was called in to coach the staff of a bank. They were completely demoralized and struggled to come into work every day because their manager had given them a mandate: "The customer is always right." This meant that no matter how demanding or abusive a customer might be, the teller had to put up with it and remain polite and businesslike.

As you might expect, the atmosphere at the bank was not a pleasant one. When a customer was unhappy, they felt free to vent their upset on the tellers. Meanwhile, the manager remained safely in his office, away from the fray.

It became very clear to me as, I worked with the staff and then with the manager, that a primary cause of their problem was a lack of clear boundaries. Thrivers establish boundaries to protect themselves from experiences that might interfere with their goals, tasks, and sense of well-being. Boundaries are not about holding yourself aloof from others or avoiding contact with them. They are about how you expect to be treated by them. Boundaries are also about insisting that this quality of respect be met—if an interaction is to continue.

In essence, a boundary is a "No"—it's about what you will *not* let someone say or do to you. But for many people, "No" is a very hard word to invoke—and make stick. Many people have been raised to believe that they do not have the right—or the ability—to establish clear boundaries and set realistic limits for someone's behavior toward them. This then sets limits on what they can accomplish for themselves—and certainly on their enjoyment of life.

How can you possibly take 100% responsibility for your life when everybody else is disregarding your needs and encroaching on your space? In truth, when you do not set and hold clear boundaries, you may end up taking responsibility for other people, while neglecting your responsibility to yourself.

How can we step into a place of gratitude and appreciation for our life when other people are pulling at us in a variety of ways? It's next to impossible to honor and nurture our spirituality when others do not respect our boundaries (and we allow that to continue).

In many ways, it is boundaries that create the space for us to live a thriving life. If we don't set and maintain clear boundaries, we end up with the scraps of our time and energy left over at the end of the day. So boundaries are about creating a space around us in which we can live our life with energy, intention, and self-respect.

Don't Fence Me In

Where my family used to live, many of the backyards were separated by waist high fences so all of them were visible and accessible to everyone else. Each fence had a gate and when it was closed, it signified a clear boundary that others respected. We knew not to enter without the owner's permission.

At first, our family liked to keep our gate open as a friendly invitation to our neighbors to come visit us. However, when a neighbor's dog made himself way too "at home" in our yard, we saw the need to keep the gate closed.

A boundary is like an invisible fence that delineates your private space. With strong boundaries, you get to choose who to allow into your space and when. No one should enter without your permission. Some people seem oblivious to the boundaries of others. And that's why it's so important to set reasonable, appropriate consequences for when a clear boundary that you have established and communicated—gets violated. The question is—how do you do that.

Boundaries are Necessary to Thrive

Have you ever been around someone who has a quality of self-respect and dignity about them that silently communicates to others how they are to be treated? If so, you'll notice that almost no one trespasses on that person's invisible boundaries. The energy of that person's presence actually calls forth good behavior from others—without their having to say a word. Someone might overstep their boundaries. But most people understand how this person is to be treated, implicitly.

Chances are, such a person has been setting limits and monitoring their boundaries long enough for them to become internalized. Then, they don't have to be defensive or self-protective because they non-verbally protect their dominion over their own space.

Many people, however, haven't yet reached that point of stability and solidity. Many are not clear what boundaries actually are or where to draw the line with other people. Others don't even feel they have the right to draw a line. Few people are raised with a healthy sense of boundaries -- and permission to set them.

Fortunately, all of us can outgrow our past limitations. We can learn to recognize and protect our value as a person so that we can use the time we have on Earth to develop and express ourselves ever more authentically. This is precisely what thriving is all about.

What Boundaries Are Not

Physical violence is clearly a boundary violation. So is emotional violence, like bullying, name calling, and any other treatment that is harmful in some way and disrespectful of the other person. Personally, I also consider being yelled at as a direct boundary violation. The manager at the bank where I was called in as a coach had a different view of things—and the results of that view were devastating to his staff's morale.

Being ordered around, threatened, pushed or hit are more obvious boundary violations. Yet many people have become so accustomed to such violations that they may feel they don't deserve to be treated any better. Is it a boundary violation for someone to call them a derogatory name, they may wonder? Is it a boundary violation for somebody to insist that they do their work for them? Where do you draw those lines? What should you just put up with to avoid a bigger hassle?

Before we answer these questions, let's discuss what boundaries are not. For one thing, boundaries are not about controlling other people. That's a misperception that some people have about boundaries. Once, in the second week of a workshop on boundaries I was conducting at a church, a participant stormed up to me and said, "This boundary thing doesn't work!" I asked her, "What do you mean it doesn't work?" She said, "I did those boundaries to my husband and it didn't change anything." I had to step back and ask her what she was trying to accomplish with her boundaries. She told me—"I'm trying to make him be a better person."

That's *not* what boundaries are about. **Boundaries are about what you will and will *not* let someone say and do to you.** It's about stopping someone from treating you badly, not trying to change their behavior in general—because you can't. All you can do is insist that you be treated with respect. And we'll discuss how to make that boundary stick in just a moment.

Another thing a boundary is not is a demand. It's not, "You will do this." It is really, "You may not do that to me." Whenever a boundary becomes a demand, you're actually trying to direct someone else rather than protect yourself. A boundary is never done to the other person, it's a line you draw that makes clear what you will not allow to have happen to you.

Boundaries are not meant to be strategies for avoiding difficult interactions. They can help you moderate difficult conversations and interactions, but not avoid them. Where would the growth be in that? Sometimes people create boundaries whenever they see an argument coming, even if the argument is about something that really does need to be addressed. Hiding behind a boundary is not the reason for a boundary. Protecting yourself from boundary violations is the reason. A boundary is meant to create the rules of engagement, not to prevent engagement.

Boundaries can help you have those difficult interactions, because it leaves you feeling safer. When you are confident in setting and holding a boundary, you can feel safe that you will be fine, regardless of the content of the interaction. You have built your own fence, and can close the gate when necessary.

Boundaries are also not standards. A standard is what you expect of yourself (we will discuss this shortly). It's something you desire to live up to. I might have a standard in which I commit to being honest with everyone around me. That's my commitment—and I can't impose it on anybody else.

A boundary can't be something I have no control over. I can't say to somebody, "You have to be honest with everybody with whom you interact." Mainly because I have no way of enforcing that. That person can walk around the corner and be dishonest with everyone that person meets. And I can't change that. What I can say is, "If you lie to me, there will be consequences." That's very different than saying, "You have to be honest with everyone." That's not something I can control.

Many times, parents put their standards on their children and treat them like boundaries. If I say to my child, "You may not lie to me. If you do, you're going to be in big trouble," that's something I can enforce (at least when I catch the dishonesty). But if I say to my child, "You have to be honest with everyone around you," there's no way I can monitor or enforce that. I can model fairness and honesty in my dealings with everyone. I can speak about why I believe this is such an important quality. But I can't coerce my child into following my lead. Boundaries have to be within our control and about us—not the other person.

Drawing Boundaries

Unfortunately, recognizing that you deserve to be treated well is not enough to get other people to respect your boundaries. So, here are five important points about boundaries that can help you draw "a line in the sand" that other people can clearly see.

#1: Your boundaries are your responsibility, not that of someone else. Sometimes people tell me that they don't understand why someone is mistreating them. I usually ask, "Have you told them yet that they can't?" Someone may cross your boundary, but it is up to you to put an end to this violation.

#2: Your boundary is not about controlling someone. As already mentioned, controlling another person is simply not possible. So, boundaries are to protect *you* by making clear what you will *and will not* tolerate from others in their interactions with you. If you've allowed someone to treat you badly in the past, but now would like them to treat you with kindness and respect, it's up to you to communicate that to them,\ and then to follow through with consequences if they don't. Otherwise, it's not a boundary yet—it's just a desire. Desires, of course, are very important. They help you determine the direction and expectations you have for your life. But you'll need boundaries to protect your goals and desires.

#3: Boundaries help you manage your emotional state. Without boundaries, it's almost impossible to feel safe and free to pursue your dreams. It can even be difficult to know what those dreams actually are. If you're afraid that someone is going to invade your space at any moment, it's all but impossible to live your life in ways that will fulfill your heart. When your boundaries are clear and firm, then you can engage more authentically with others.

#4: Boundaries must be repeatedly communicated: When you're setting boundaries with someone who is accustomed to disregarding you in one way or another, don't expect them to get the message right away. Boundaries must be repeatedly stated until they are actually accepted by others. It rarely works to say to someone once, "Hey, it's not okay for you to raise your voice at me." You more likely have to say it each time that person does what you don't want them to do—until they finally get the message. True boundaries are the ones you repeat and reinforce until they become lodged in other people's thinking. Only then is the boundary real, set, and held.

#5: Boundaries become a part of you the more you practice them. Setting a boundary—repeatedly—helps you become more comfortable with what's okay and what's not okay when it comes to how you're treated. The more we accept our own boundaries as legitimate and appropriate, the less we have to mention them to others. That's because, like people with dignity and self-respect, these boundaries eventually simply emanate from us. Until that happens, however, we have to be prepared to state what our boundaries are until we actually believe in them and insist upon them—and the other person does, too. Until that happens, the boundary is still in process.

How to Set a Boundary & Make It Stick

Now let's look at the four steps required to set boundaries that stick in your own mind and the minds of other people.

Step 1: Inform

Inform the other person of what they're doing that isn't okay with you. Let's go back to the example of the bank. My instruction to the tellers was to let the customer know when their words or tone were rude—but to do it diplomatically, so the upset doesn't escalate.

For instance, if a customer was yelling at the teller, the teller could say in a neutral and respectful voice, "Do you realize that you're raising your voice with me?" By stating it as "raising your voice," they avoid getting into a debate about the definition of yelling. They're simply making an observation that the customer is speaking loudly—not issuing a judgment about it. I challenged the tellers not to take the customer's aggressive tone personally, but to respond in a mellow way, as if they were saying something as innocuous as, "Do you realize that the sky is blue?" They're just establishing what happened—not meeting fire with fire.

This same approach can be used for a variety of issues. You might say to a co-worker, "Are you aware that you keep pushing your work onto me?" Or, "Do you realize that you keep coming over to my desk and taking stuff from it?"

Now there's an inference in this approach that the other person is unaware of how they're violating your boundaries. This is a good place to begin, because it gives the other person a graceful way of backing off. In the case of the tellers, their neutral way of communicating to the customer that they're actually raising their voice, can defuse the situation right there. The person could immediately say, "Oh, I'm so sorry, I'm upset, but didn't mean to be yelling at you." Then, it's possible to have a normal conversation. Of course, the other person could respond in another way—like, "You know what? I meant to be yelling at you." This then takes us to step number two.

Step 2: Ask
If the teller gets a pushback from the customer, they then can say—again, in a neutral tone—"Please do not raise your voice at me." The customer now has a choice of responding differently. They can lower their voice and say, "I'm so sorry, I just want to deal with this quickly." Or, they might keep going in that tone and say, "I'll yell at you if I want to." Which then leads to step number three.

Step 3: Demand
A demand sounds something like this, "You may not raise your voice at me." What makes it possible for you to stay calm and use a neutral tone—instead of yelling back—is the step that follows the demand that someone honor your boundaries. You've progressed from informing, to asking, to demanding. At that point, the customer has the choice to continue on in the way they've been acting or to change tactics. Many customers recognize at that point that they're dealing with somebody who is self-assured, self-respecting, and unwilling to be treated rudely.

Step 4: Consequence
At the bank, the consequence was simply expressed this way, "If you continue to raise your voice with me, our conversation will be over and I will refer you to our manager." This is how the teller can protect a boundary. And now it was time for the manager to step up to the challenge and set his own boundaries.

As you'll recall, he'd been hiding out in his office and leaving the problem customers to the tellers because he didn't want to be yelled at, either. So, I helped him to establish *his* boundaries, so he could take a leadership position with his staff.

It's very important to note that a consequence is not a punishment. It's a strategy for self-protection. But it has to be enforced or it won't be effective.

Let's say you're having a conversation with an angry friend. You may follow the four steps of the process and find it is necessary to end the conversation. Ending the conversation is not a punishment. It's a clear statement that you're not willing to be treated rudely. You may then decide that you need an hour apart, or two hours, a day apart, or even a week apart or more. Whatever it is, that consequence has to be something that's not meant as a punishment but as a way of you protecting yourself.

You also have to ask yourself the question, "What is going to be the effect of this consequence—on me and the other person? Am I going to be able to carry it out? Is it in balance with the boundary violation? Or am I now violating the sanctity of my friend's space by saying something like, 'If you yell at me, I am never ever, for the rest of my life, going to speak to you again. And I am going to tell everybody we know what a horrible person you are.'"

I've purposefully exaggerated it to make the point that the consequence needs to be appropriate and readily enacted. In this case, it's clearly not. So you have to take a look at whether such a consequence is fair and also whether you can follow through on it. To state a consequence that is out of balance or unenforceable is to lose credibility and make your words sound hollow in the ears of other people.

(Consider the father of a family headed off on a vacation telling the quarreling children in the back seat, "If you don't stop, I'm turning this car around and we're going home." Not a person in the car—perhaps even the father—believes this. So it only serves to reduce his credibility.)

Determining appropriate consequences for an infringement of your clearly stated, firmly established, boundaries is essential. In the case of the bank tellers, they were able to say, "Our conversation will be complete and you can take up your complaint with the branch manager if you're unable to speak civilly to me." Now notice that they did not say, "You can never come to my teller station again, you can never deal with me again, I will never talk to you again." It was simply that if the customer could not stop berating the teller, then he or she could continue their conversation with the manager.

As already mentioned, before a consequence gets enacted, the person who has violated a boundary has had a chance in the **Demand** to back down. The teller communicates, "You may not yell at me, you may not raise your voice at me, if you continue to do so our conversation will be over." They weren't suddenly throwing out that consequence. They were announcing that they would not continue with the conversation.

What you're trying to do is teach people how to treat you and stay in relationship with you. That's what boundaries allow us to do. And we set them up by **Informing** the person about the behavior, **Asking** that the boundary be honored, then **Demanding** that it is—and then enacting the **Consequence,** if it isn't.

Here's what that it looks like: #1: "Do you realize that you're raising your voice at me?" #2: "Please do not raise your voice with me." #3: "You may not raise your voice at me. If you continue, we will end this conversation and you can speak with the manager." #4: "This conversation is over. Let me show you to our manager."

These are the steps you can apply to set boundaries anywhere in your life. However, there are times when there is a need for an immediate response. In such a case, you go straight for the consequence. If there is violence, you don't take time to go through the steps. If someone is hitting you, you can simply say, "We're done," and walk away and/or call for help. That's the immediate consequence. In this case, it may be very appropriate to say, "I'm never going to speak with you again"—or whatever it takes to protect yourself and feel safe again. That's first and foremost!

When Free Coaching Comes Your Way

Let's say that someone is verbally abusing or insulting you—face-to-face, over the phone, or by email. You have options. You can absolutely refuse to continue the communication. But you might also want to ask yourself the question, "Is any of what they're saying valid? What part of this is true and possibly helpful for me to hear—despite the unpleasantness with which it is being communicated?"

One of my coaches received some rather harshly given criticism from a client, which was certainly disturbing in the moment. But ultimately, she decided to look upon it as free coaching. She chose to disregard what felt like a personal attack and simply sift through the message for any useful feedback. That's a really mature and useful strategy for dealing with what may at first sound only like a verbal attack.

On the other hand, if the critical words do not contain any useful insights—they're just an angry insult from someone in your life—then you can do what my mother always suggests, "Consider the source." That makes it easier not to take it personally. You realize that these are just angry words coming from somebody who is dealing with their own stuff. It's not really about you at all. This individual is projecting their upset upon you; but like someone trained in martial arts, you can simply step out of the range of their attack.

You might say to yourself, "That's about them, not about me. I'm not going to let it in. I'm just letting it go." This protects you. It may also put you into a more compassionate, less angry space. Being able to let go and forgive, are essential for thriving—regardless of what is going on around us.

The four steps we have covered are external boundaries, where you stop the words or actions from getting to you. What we are now discussing is an "internal boundary," for how far you let someone's words or behaviors get inside you. It is not enough to have external boundaries. Internal boundaries keep those hurts and insults from affecting you.

We have to take leadership over our mind, protect ourselves from the negativity that is all around us, and also refuse to let our own thoughts get the best of us. It's essential that we protect ourselves externally as well as internally from negativity.

That Bank?

So, what happened at the bank? As you can imagine, the manager was quite busy for a few weeks, because the difficult customers had gotten into a bad habit of making demands and mistreating the staff. Customers had learned to bully their way to get what they wanted, fair or not.

The manager and I had long talks about how to manage these irate customers and what the appropriate consequences would be. At some point, the manager might have to say, "You know, I'm not sure if this bank is a good fit for you as a customer." Some of the worst offenders did leave the bank. But most of the previously difficult people began to realize that they needed to handle their upset more consciously and respectfully. The staff was not there to absorb their stress or give them everything they wanted.

It didn't take long before the tellers were treated with greater respect, the atmosphere at the bank improved, and the employees felt better about coming to work. Now that their boundaries were well defined, customers no longer came in with the expectation that they could vent their financial stress on the people who were endeavoring to serve them. Boundaries were clear and everyone thrived. Your task, as someone who is intent on thriving, is to be constantly strengthening and monitoring your boundaries so that the people in your life will treat you in the respectful way that you want and deserve to be treated.

Interestingly, in this branch office, I helped the manager understand that it cost the bank more to have bad customers than to attract good ones. The "higher ups" were quite happy to see a happy staff and a flow of new customers. As it turned out, they attracted what they accepted. Since they were willing to allow their boundaries to be crossed, they found customers quite willing to do that.

That is true with boundaries. We attract people at the level we are willing to set and hold our boundaries.

TL;DR—Maintain Boundaries

- Boundaries protect you from the actions of others. They mark the place where you end, and what you will accept. Boundaries are a "No" to others: "No, I will not do that," and "No, you may not do that."

- It is impossible to fully say "Yes" to life, unless you can say "No" to something encroaching upon you. Otherwise, you won't feel safe.

- Boundaries are not manipulation of others. You don't "Do a boundary to someone." You set a boundary, not so that the other person has to do something, but so they do not treat you in ways you do not want to be treated.

- Boundaries are not a way to avoid difficult interactions, but a way to make those interactions productive. Boundaries are not demands of how the other person must be, but how they must treat you. So, the boundary has to be in your control.

- Boundaries are YOUR responsibility. It is up to you to set (and hold) your boundaries. The other person may not immediately want to honor your boundaries, so they must be repeatedly stated (and enforced).

- There are four steps to setting a boundary (unless there is violence, and then the response is to immediately leave and get safe).

  1. Inform—Let the other person know they are crossing a boundary. For example: "Do you realize you are raising your voice at me?"

  2. Ask—If the person continues to violate your boundary, you ask them to stop. For example: "Please do not raise your voice at me."

  3. Demand—If the person continues, you demand the violation stop, and let the person know there is a consequence. For example, "You may not raise your voice at me. If you continue, I will leave for a couple of hours."

  4. Consequence—If the person persists in crossing your boundary, you carry out the consequence you threatened.

- Two key points: First, maintain a neutral tone, flat tone. Second, refrain from crossing the person's boundary in the process of setting your boundary.

Chapter 10

raise your standards

a s we discussed in the previous chapter, a boundary is a "No" directed toward other people. Whether spoken or unspoken, it serves as an invisible barrier that we erect to protect our personal space from the unwanted encroachments of other people.

By contrast, a *Standard* is a "Yes" we place upon ourselves as an intention and expectation for our own behavior. Standards are morals, ethics, principles, traits, and supportive habits that we admire and aim to embody. They are agreements we make with ourselves on who we want to be and how we want to interact in the world.

Clearly, everyone needs both boundaries and standards to thrive in the world. We create boundaries to protect and free ourselves—to rise up and become our ever-better Selves. We set standards as the way to rise up.

Standards are not the same as rules. Rules and laws are created by others as behaviors that we must follow—or face the consequences. They are external structures. By contrast, personal standards are our own creation. And failing to live up to them may—or may not—carry any significant *external* consequences.

However, when we let ourselves "off the hook"—instead of fulfilling our own standards—we do have a personal price to pay.

When it comes to personal standards, cutting corners cuts into self-esteem. The late psychotherapist Nathaniel Branden, known for his pioneering work on the psychology of self-esteem, pointed out that positive self-esteem is more than just positive self-regard. It is composed of the good feelings we have about ourselves *because of* the good stuff we're doing in the world. People who live up to their own high standards—as the means to fulfill their greater potential—earn their own self-respect as well as the respect of others.

Thrivers strive to fulfill their standards—day in and day out—no matter what. They don't just talk about them. In fact, they may not speak of them at all. More likely, they just go about meeting their own internal expectations without any witnesses and behind closed doors.

If somebody says, "I'm an honest person," but is willing to fudge on their taxes, or cut corners in their dealings with other people, then they are deceiving themselves in the process. And over time, the distance between what they profess to uphold and what they actually do in private can have a corrosive impact on their sense of self.

A person may justify lowering their standards on occasion with excuses like, "Everybody does it," or "I'm just cheating the cheaters." But allowing something on the outside to compromise the internal standards that we desire and profess to live by can cause us to feel—consciously or unconsciously—like we're not such a good person after all. In fact, we feel the disingenuousness. And that feeling undermines not only our self-esteem but also our ability to withstand the "stress tests" that life is forever imposing on us. Over time, being true to our standards builds our character and inner strength. It lets us know that we will always come through for our selves and for those we love and support.

In reality, those difficult times give us the opportunity to live out standards we have already chosen. They are tests of our commitment to the standard and opportunities to raise our standards.

Standards happen silently and become a way of life. They are what kicks in when the going gets tough. For instance, when we're looking at those taxes, and there's just not enough money to pay them—we still don't fudge the figures.

Or, when someone points out an error that we've made and we know that they are right, we don't try to hide behind an excuse. We tell the truth. We take responsibility. We apologize. We also forgive ourselves and resolve anew to do better next time.

Thrivers are people who are constantly raising their standards—at the same time that they're strengthening their boundaries. By so doing, they are creating the space that enables them to constantly become more of who they really are, instead of settling for a lesser version of themselves. There's always more within us than we know. And the more we take responsibility for our lives, and strive to exceed our own last best efforts, the more we become authentic expressions of our true self.

In order to consistently live up to our own standards, Thrivers take increasing responsibility for their own lives. They're too busy living up to their personal expectations to want to play games with other people. And by meeting these expectations, thrivers hold a quality of being that inspires people to treat them with respect.

That's one of the ways that personal standards reinforce personal boundaries. The stronger your boundaries are, the higher you can raise your standards. The higher your standards go, the more you're going to see the places where you need to have a stronger boundary. Standards and Boundaries are like the two wings of a bird. They enable Thrivers to fly.

Life constantly challenges us to learn, grow, and develop, so that with age may come not just wrinkles but wisdom and compassion toward ourselves and others, as well. To live without one or the other is to live a restricted life.

Our greatest legacy—our greatest gift to our family, friends and the future— is the person we become in the time we have to be here. And as we continue to evolve throughout our lives, we become ever more sensitive to the unpleasantness we create when we shrink from our responsibilities and reduce our standards because of a lack of inner strength in the face of outer challenges. We begin to see the consequences of what happens when we don't hold our standards, when we don't hold our boundaries.

Thrivers frequently ask themselves, "How can I raise my standards to a new level? In what areas can I reasonably expect more of myself?" The higher your standards, the more the people around you will be drawn to you and will respect and admire you. As thrivers continue to elevate their standards and maintain their boundaries, they shape their identities as people who follow their own North Star.

By raising our standards and clarifying our boundaries, we make it clear to other people how we are to be treated. We also make a statement to ourselves that we are a person of value and integrity striving for ever-greater authenticity.

People can cover themselves in expensive things to indicate their wealth. But high standards, lived with consistency, convey a level of inner wealth that can never be purchased by anything other than the daily work of living up to our own high standards, day by day, year after year. This is what shows the true worth of a person.

How To Raise Your Standards

So how do you identify the standards that mean the most to you? You can begin by looking around at what you think are the most important traits in life. I recommend that you write them down. We've already discussed honesty. But what is important to you? What qualities stand out for you in the people you've admired at different times in your life? We often identify the values we most want by the values we admire in others.

Next, think about the degree to which you currently live up to these traits that you admire. In some cases you may be able to say, "That's exactly me. That's something that I treasure, and that's something that I do and am." In some cases, you may recognize certain standards that the heroes in your life have embodied—like perseverance, optimism, and a sense of humor in the face of major challenges. These may once have seemed out of reach to you. If so, then you have begun to identify areas in which you'd like to grow.

Some people are so committed to a standard, that it can almost get them into trouble. One of my beloved mother-in-law's core standards was loyalty. If she was on your side, she was on your side no matter what. She would defend you from detractors as much as she could because that was her standard. Could it get her in trouble? Absolutely. You can show loyalty to someone who does not deserve it.

My father has the great capacity of always thinking the best of others. That is a beautiful trait and a wonderful standard. But every now and then, someone may just take advantage of you. But I have come to realize that, on the balance, he does not live his life expecting someone to take advantage. When it happens, he brushes it off and again believes in the best. And he holds himself to a standard of treating others the very best he can.

Sometimes, people are going to let you down. Sometimes, people are not what they seem. People can fall short. But my mother-in-law saw loyalty as such an important standard that she would always be loyal to those around her. My father believes in the best in people, and treats people accordingly.

Begin to think about the top ten traits that you value most in another person. Usually, what we most value in a friend or mentor are the standards by which they live because this contributes to the quality of their being. Now, turn around and ask yourself, "To what degree am I living up to these standards?"

Maybe it's loyalty, or honesty; maybe it's kindness or a perpetually loving spirit. Maybe it's somebody who always fulfills what they say they're going to do. If you find these standards important in a friend, you probably are going to think they're pretty important for you to live by, too. Whether you're living them out now or not doesn't matter. You're still pointing to those standards in your own life. And by so doing, you can set your intention and direction for the future.

Now look at how you can raise your standards—how you can take them up a notch. If you say, "I think it's important to always be honest with other people," then think about how you can be more consistently honest. Can you identify the places where you'd like to strengthen that trait?

There's always a higher level to which a standard can be raised. There's always another place to grow into. And that's the thing about thriving. It's about growing into higher, bigger, and better standards for yourself. It's actually fun to challenge yourself in this way. And there's a huge pay-off in terms of how you feel about yourself, how you function in the world, and how you are seen by others.

Now, once you have your list of ten traits that are important to you, and ten traits that you value in a friend, you'll notice that there is a lot of overlap. So, look at the standards that stand out as the most important to you and pick only one or two standards to work on to begin with. Don't try to go after all of them. We can always bring in additional standards and raise the standards we have as we progress.

For this experiment, start with one or two. Then, ask yourself the question, "To what degree am I living that today?" If you were rating yourself, what would your percentage of consistency be? Are you at one hundred percent—or ninety, eighty, seventy, sixty? In that way, you may well be able to see where there's room for growth.

Sometimes people discover that—though they thought they were living one of their standards 100% of the time—in actual fact, there's still room to grow beyond that. Wherever you are, begin to say, "How can I raise it up to the next level?" Just choose one or two standards and remember that standards are habits you are building. If you want to raise your standards, you have to form a new habit and maintain it for at least a couple of months until it becomes automatic and effortless

An easy way to do this is to track it day by day. Every morning—or better yet, just before bed—consider how you will practice and elevate the two standards you are focusing on throughout the day. You can combine this exercise with the daily writing you do in your gratitude journal. You can start each morning—and/or at the end of each day—by asking yourself, "What are the things for which I am feeling especially grateful?" Then, ask yourself, "What are a couple of things I can do today to reach a higher standard?" Then, at the end of the day, as you're reviewing your gratitude journal and looking for more things to appreciate, you can ask yourself the question, "How did I do today? Did I live it out the way I wanted to?"

This is not your chance to judge or criticize yourself. It's your chance to ask, "How did I do today? I'll get a fresh start tomorrow. What can I do to achieve a higher level?" It is a chance to simply reflect on where you have been, re-set your intentions, and begin the process again.

You have to be vigilant to prevent your thoughts from getting you down. No matter how well you did, you could always do better. So when you take inventory, give yourself a lot of credit for what went well. And don't spend too much time focusing on what didn't. You can say, "The past is done. I'm going to let go of what happened today. Some things went well, and that's great. Some things didn't go so well. But I'm going to continue working on it. I'm going to go to the next level and tomorrow, I'm going to do better." Then, think about how you can do that.

We get a fresh start each day to live at a higher standard, to reinforce our boundaries, and improve our overall quality of life. Take advantage of that. In the morning, think about how you're going to live out that day. In the evening, review how you did. Give yourself credit for your achievements. And give yourself compassion for the areas where you fell short. This is not a time to say, "Bad me, poor me." It's a chance to say, "I will do better tomorrow. I can live up to a higher standard tomorrow. This is my opportunity to grow." (More on growth later.)

As you do that, you'll notice that slowly your standards begin to grow. Then, after you've enhanced the two qualities or behaviors that you've chosen, go back and pick another one or two. After you're living those at a higher level, and they're pretty much cemented in with habits that support them, then pick another two. What you will quickly discover is that you've joined the Thrivers by being a person who continually raises your standards to the next level. There's nothing sweeter in life than steadily becoming one's own best self.

TL;DR—Raise Your Standards

- If Boundaries are a "NO" to how others treat you, Standards are a "YES" to what you expect of yourself. For example, "I will be fair and honest with everyone I encounter."
- Standards are not rules and laws, which are externally created and enforced. Standards are internal decisions you make and follow.
- Standards always have a place to be raised, a place to be lived into more fully and more consistently. Thrivers seek to raise their standards, and then live them. Practice is the only way to raise and improve standards.
- You can discover new standards for yourself by noticing the traits you admire in others. And you can also see the places for stronger standards by the values you already hold for yourself.

Chapter 11

care for yourself

a number of years ago, I was involved in the creation of a video on how people in family-owned businesses could deal more effectively with the family issues that invariably arise. I totally exhausted myself over the course of several days of planning and then appearing on camera. By the end of the process, late on a Sunday afternoon, I was exhausted.

When I woke up the next day, unsurprisingly, I felt truly worn out. By Tuesday, the exhaustion—rather than lessening—had turned into a feeling of overall ill health. My back hurt and, as the week progressed, the pain spread down my legs and up my back.

I was sure that this was the result of all the concentrated days of filming and the demands this placed on my mind and body. I was certain I'd recover from the stress in the next little while. But what happened, instead, is that the feeling of not being okay continued to grow and spread. Clearly, something wasn't right with me.

As the days progressed, it got harder and harder for me to move around. So, about a week and a half later, my wife finally said, "That's it, Honey. You've got to go see the doctor." And thus began a harrowing journey through a completely unexpected brush with my mortality.

It took six weeks before the doctors could figure out what was wrong with me. When they finally did, the answer they gave us was devastating. They expected me to be permanently disabled, followed by an early death at some point. Fortunately, although the diagnosis was accurate, the prognosis was not. I was given another chance at life.

Dying to Live

The illness had been a wake-up call. But wake up to what? That's what I was about to find out.

After six or seven months of recuperation, my wife gave me a gift of something I had always wanted to do, but had put off for years: scuba diving. When I was at my sickest, I thought I'd never be able to do anything strenuous and exciting like that again. It felt like a miracle that now I actually could.

At the first scuba class, the instructor had us swim three laps of a large pool. That means up and back six times. I managed to complete the swim. But when I dragged myself out of the water and stood by the instructor, I said to him, "If you were trying to demonstrate that we need to get in better shape, I really got the message." He smiled, and the next day, I went to the gym. That started a process in which I began taking care of my body in a way I'd never done before.

When I look back at a photo of myself from that time—holding my now college-age (but then small) son in my arms—it's hard to believe that the person in the photo is actually me. I look soft, overweight, and unhealthy. How ironic. In all those years of focusing on thriving, I hadn't been paying much attention to my body. It would send me occasional distress signals. But I basically ignored them—until I no longer could. As my life-threatening illness demonstrated to me, I needed to support my physical well-being in every way possible if I intended to fulfill my mental, emotional, and spiritual aspirations.

How obvious this was. And yet, what a revelation. I've since noticed that many people in the self-help field make the same mistake by focusing on the mind—all the while taking their health for granted. As long as everything is working well, it's easy to overlook the fact that what allows us to have a thriving life is a thriving body. This doesn't mean that we have a washboard stomach or qualify for the cover of "Health" magazine. It just means that we have to treat our bodies well and give them what they need so that we can thrive mentally, emotionally, spiritually—and physically, first and foremost.

So at the risk of stating the obvious, let me just share what my illness taught me: When our body is not in good shape, we get tired more easily. We lose some of our mobility. Therefore, we can't be of service to our loved ones and our community to the degree that we would like. As I learned the hard way, we ignore the body at our peril. If it's not thriving, it's not capable of taking us where we want to go. Your body has to take your mind, your soul, and the rest of you through the world. Simple as that.

The Brain in the Belly

We've all heard about the relationship of serotonin levels in the brain with feelings of wellbeing or depression. But did you know that scientists have discovered that we have more neurotransmitters in our gut than we do in our brain? In fact, we actually have a brain in our gut. In some ways, our whole being is involved in our neural structure and, thus, with our moods. So, if we're not taking care of our physical health, we're not going to feel as well as we could overall. And that's not something you can fix with a pill.

In a sense, taking good care of ourselves is a form of service we perform in the world, because it extends our useful life and our capacity to be of service to others. How did I fail to see this—until my health almost failed me completely? Fortunately, I did finally catch on before it was too late. And I've since been able to identify four key factors that can make it possible for almost anyone to restore and maintain good health—providing they practice these factors consistently.

Despite what the media tells us, being fit and healthy really has nothing to do with rippling muscles, a washboard stomach, or the ability to fit into the "ideal" size for the "perfect" man or woman. It's not about living up to anyone else's ideal of the perfect body. It's just about taking such good care of your own body that it will allow you to fulfill your greater potential in the world.

You don't have to live up to anyone else's ideal of the perfect body. You don't even have to achieve "optimal health," according to someone else's standards. I'm just suggesting that you find what is optimal and do-able for *you*. What enables you to bring your best self to your family and community?

When we're not in a healthy place, we're not able to make as positive an impact—or to sustain it. We're also limited in our pursuit of meaning and purpose in life. In fact, it's really difficult to even take full responsibility for our lives when our body isn't as healthy as it could be.

When we've lost our good health, it can take a lot of time, money, and people to help us get it back. So, the best way we can avoid all that is to stay in good health throughout our lives—to the degree possible—by adopting these four easy practices for achieving a healthy, well-functioning body.

The Four Keys to Good Health

Based on my own experience, I believe that our bodies are quite resilient. I believe that they're capable of coming back from a lot. I've seen my own body heal and find a new way of being once I changed a few key things.

I want to provide some basic guidelines that are easy to implement, and give you the "biggest bang for your buck." From there, you can begin to focus on areas of interest and leanings. One thing you will note is that as you begin caring for one area of your health, you begin to naturally make better choices in other areas. As you respect yourself and your health, your level of self-care begins to grow, leading to increasing health and increasing self-respect.

Here are your four targets:

Target 1: Rest

Our bodies need to recharge and recover every night. A recovery period allows our brains to process the day's experiences, store information in long-term memory, and recalibrate for the next day.

Most research shows that, generally speaking, we need somewhere between seven and nine hours of sleep. Of course, some people need more and some less, but that's the median range. It's not hard to know whether you're getting enough sleep or not. If your body wakes up naturally, and you feel ready to tackle another day, then you're likely meeting your needs for rest.

Unfortunately, many people believe that they can burn themselves out during the week, and then recharge on weekends. It's a pattern many people establish in their teen and college years. But research shows that you can't just bounce back from a week of sleep deprivation by getting 18 hours of sleep on a Saturday.

Consistency across the board is what it takes to establish and maintain good health. Seven to nine hours a night is a good goal to aim toward and certain strategies can help you more readily achieve that goal. One strategy is to establish and follow a regular bedtime routine.

Preparing for a Good Night's Rest: Our bodies are designed to wind down and get rest when the sun goes down. So, what happens when it's always light—inside and out? How does that perpetual light affect our body's natural rhythms?

We live in a world that extends day into night. City lights that keep us from seeing the stars—along with all our electronic devices—create the illusion of a day that never ends. Specifically, the blue light emitted by televisions and other electronic devices has been shown to trick the brain into thinking it still needs to stay awake.

Research is showing more and more clearly that the blue light emitted from electronics is exactly the lighting that most alerts the body that it is time to be awake. In other words, the devices we typically have in hand at the end of the day are creating exactly the type of illumination that is telling you it is time to be alert and work.

So, the first thing I would recommend is that you create a routine where you get away from these light sources. Try putting away the tablets, smart phones, and other devices a couple of hours before bedtime. That way, you not only avoid the brain-confusion caused by the blue light, but you also stop the mental processing that comes with answering emails and other related activities that we engage in all day long. The mind needs a chance to wind down. Albert Einstein played violin in the evenings to give his mind a rest and prepare his body for sleep.

Stimulants: Another way to make sure your body is primed for relaxation at bedtime is to limit your consumption of stimulants—like caffeine and sugar, especially toward the end of the day. A lot of times people get a craving late at night for a soft drink, coffee, hot chocolate, or tea, which generally contain either or both caffeine and sugar—or a chemical substitute. They may also want a sweet treat. But all these substances rev up the body. That's why I recommend avoiding stimulants of all kinds at least two hours before bed. It is a good way to help your body let go.

For some sensitive people, the effects of caffeine can last for hours. If you find yourself getting a bit jittery or wired from your coffee, cola, or tea, you may need to leave out those drinks from mid-afternoon on, just to make sure you have processed the caffeine by bedtime.

Keep in mind that decaffeinated coffee or tea doesn't mean that they have no caffeine—it just means they have less caffeine. So, that's an important area to look at if you have a hard time calming down when you go to bed.

At the other end of the chemical spectrum, many people think an evening drink (or drinks) of beer, wine, or other alcohol helps them to calm down and get to sleep. Unfortunately, while it may seem to have that effect, brain activity is disrupted by alcohol, leading to less-than-optimal sleep. If at all possible, avoid alcohol before bedtime. And any alcohol use in the evening should be light, to avoid disrupting your sleep.

It's also very helpful to make sure your bedroom is completely dark when you're ready for sleep—and stays dark after dawn. Closing the door to block out the light, and using shades or curtains that completely darken the room, will make a significant difference to the quality of your rest. In addition to a darker room—cooler is also better. Such conditions support deeper rest.

Bedtime Routines: As parents, we create bedtime routines for our children. Generally speaking, we give them a bath, put on their pajamas, read them a story, and tuck them into bed. As adults, however, we mostly forget that we have the same needs for a consistent routine to signal our body and brain that this is the time to wind down and get some sleep.

Whatever bedtime routine works for you, I would simply encourage you to add two important elements of self-care because they can make an enormous positive difference.

First, if you're not already giving yourself a few minutes of meditation and reflection time, I highly recommend it. A meditative time allows you to quiet your mind, let that jumble of busy thoughts slow down and drift away, and enjoy some deep, cleansing belly breaths that can calm your whole system. A few minutes of breathing, unwinding, and relaxing will create a greater sense of peace and compassion for yourself and others.

Second, take some time for reflection and to contemplate the many things for which you feel gratitude—even in the midst of the many challenges you may be facing. It's amazing what that change of focus can do to a person's feeling of okay-ness. By transforming the "glass" from half-empty to half-full, we give ourselves a greater sense of inner fullness, appreciation and even contentment.

Thinking about the things for which we're grateful, and then reflecting on how we can take these good feelings into our next day, brings a greater sense of thriving into our awareness. It's also a very good way to complete the day just before going to sleep.

So, all of these practices—a bedtime routine, avoiding stimulants including screen time, making sure your bedroom is dark and cool, plus evening meditation and reflection—can create a deeper state of peace, leading to a more restful and refreshing sleep.

Target 2: Exercise

Bodies are meant to stretch and move. So another important area of self-care is exercise. But I'm not talking about the kind in which you're constantly trying to build your body up or get ready for swimsuit season. What I'm referring to is that a sedentary life is not a thriving life.

Research demonstrates that the more time we spend sitting—hour after hour, day after day—the greater our chances of dying younger. This doesn't mean you should immediately invest in an adjustable standing desk. If you'll just get up and move around for five minutes every hour or so, you can help your whole body maintain health and flexibility. (I will admit that after reading the research, I did shift to a standing desk. I spend time both sitting and standing throughout the day, along with some walking.)

Think you'll lose productivity if you interrupt yourself at regular 50-55 minute increments? Actually, the opposite is true. Your mind is not capable of working effectively past that 50-minute time frame (in fact, your attention span is much shorter than that). So, you might as well get up, get out of your head, move around and shake it up a little bit. Allow your body to stretch and twist to keep your spine flexible and your joints in good working order. You may be surprised to discover how much better you feel with just a little extra movement periodically throughout the day.

It's so easy to overlook how important this is until—as in my case—you can't dismiss it any more. But regular physical exertion was the way of life for our hunter-gatherer forbearers. And our brains and bodies are essentially the same as our ancient ancestors. So, the need to integrate exercise into our daily experience is easy to see.

Our lives are in no way as arduous as theirs were. But our chronic stress levels may sometimes be greater and more persistent. Exercise is a wonderful way to stay fit and healthy and also to relieve stress. So, even if your schedule allows you less than ten minutes of workout time a few days a week, you'll be amazed at how helpful that can be to your long-term health and well-being.

For a "minimal effective dose" of exercise, you may have heard of the "Scientific Seven-Minute Workout." It is a research-based exercise routine that allows all of your body to get some attention through an interval training that includes high-intensity exercise for 30 seconds, followed by a 10-second pause before the next exercise. It doesn't require weights—just a wall and a chair.

Everyone can find seven minutes in the day. And that's a really good place to start. There are apps for pretty much every device that will lead you through this particular workout. You'll find information on-line, so give it a try.

One of the things that I realized when I was trying to get back into shape was that I needed to find some small starting point. It can feel overwhelming if you think you need to do a 45-90 minute routine. I just couldn't see myself doing that. I wish there'd been a seven-minute workout when I was first getting into shape. But now, because I've maintained my exercise regimen, I've built-up to longer work out sessions. And I truly feel better than ever.

Seven minutes can be a good starting point for you if you don't already have a routine. Then, if you add 15 minutes of walking to it, you've got a 20+ minute commitment that can actually make an enormous positive difference in your life.

If you feel unable to do a strenuous exercise, I would suggest you start with a bit of walking. In fact, I believe that everyone should walk each day. It has enormous benefits for your entire system. I am not talking about "speed walking." Simply walking at a steady pace, whatever that is for you. Shoot for 15 minutes each day, minimum and build up from there.

I use my twice-daily walk time to meditate in the morning, and then catch up with my wife in the evening when we walk together. So, while I am getting some quiet time or connection time in, I am also benefitting my body. Not a bad use of those minutes.

I'm referring to the "minimal, effective daily dosage" of exercise—unless you're inspired to do more. You don't have to go to the gym three or four hours a day, or "pump iron" several days a week, to have the quality of health and energy you need to thrive. Just take time to explore and discover for yourself what works best for your body. Then find a way to give that to yourself on a regular basis. Depending on your age, your health, your fitness, and circumstances—find out what keeps your body functioning at its best.

Target 3: Diet

The third key is diet: Being attentive to what you put into your body, nutritionally. One of the realizations I had when I was on the road to recovery was that, in a sense, my body is my vehicle. And whatever I eat becomes fuel for my physical vehicle. So the question for me became, am I putting in high-octane fuel or am I putting in low-grade fuel that could eventually clog up the pipes, tubes, and engine? Once I began looking at it that way, I realized that I wasn't burning the good stuff—which is why I was burning myself out. And so, I began to look for healthier ways to eat.

One of the frustrating things about trying to figure out how to eat well for your body is that some of the leading nutritionists disagree with each other. What's touted today as a miracle food or diet may prove tomorrow to be not all that good for us. So, after a lot of exploration for myself, my advice to you is to stay away from the gimmick diets and find your own way to improve how you eat every day.

I have chosen to eat a low-carb, lean-protein diet with a good amount of healthy fats. I also stay away from white foods—like processed flour, sugar, baked potatoes, and other starchy foods. All these carbs convert quickly to sugar in the body. And a heavy sugar load is a built-in signal to our body to store the excess calories.

It makes perfect sense that this would be so, when we look from an evolutionary perspective. In late summer and fall, starchy vegetables and fruit become prevalent. Our ancestors ate a lot of these foods to prepare for a long, cold winter. Like hibernating animals, they needed to trigger their bodies to store as much fat as possible for the lean times ahead. Feast and famine was a normal way of life for them.

Most people reading this book are free of concern for where their next meal will come from. So, a low-carb diet—along with lean, nutritious proteins (which excludes most luncheons meats)—is the kind of fuel our bodies need to run well throughout the year.

As for the healthy fats, that's been a controversial subject for a long time. Now, however, researchers have demonstrated that good fats—like coconut oil and olive oil—are highly beneficial for our bodies. Avocados and nuts also have a lot of good fat that fuels our bodies.

Let me just suggest that a healthy plate is made up of approximately two-thirds fruits and vegetables (heavy on veggies and light on fruit), one-third lean protein—and all the rest of the plate can be covered with heavy starches. If you are good at math, you already know there is no other space. So, I really recommend eliminating as much as possible those unhealthy starches from the diet—especially the kind that come in bags and are baked or fried. They may taste great, for the few seconds you taste them. But that flavor comes with a price.

Of course giving up starches and carbohydrates is not all that easy. Research has shown that these yummy comfort foods are actually addictive. So when it comes to snack foods especially, it may help to read the list of ingredients on the package—and to remind yourself that this is the fuel you're using to run your physical vehicle. Recognizing the chemical stew that has gone into making these sweet or salty taste treats can help you gain leverage over their addictive attraction. After all, it takes the best fuel to get the highest mileage and best performance out of our bodies.

A friend of mine told me something that I've adopted as I choose what I want to put in my body. He said, "I eat to live—rather than living to eat." I want to eat tasty foods—absolutely! But I want to make sure these foods are fueling my body in ways that allow me to flourish—rather than simply pleasing my taste buds but burning me out.

If you are telling yourself, "That seems like a dull meal," I assure you, my eating is much more tasty and satisfying than it was before. To be honest, my observation is that most people eat their meals completely distracted. If you focus on the taste, texture, and how you feel from the foods you eat, you will likely move in more healthy directions, naturally. That fast food meal is not so tasty. That is one reason we eat with distractions: so we don't notice. Time to notice!

Target 4: Passing the Stress Test

Much like thoughts, stress is a misunderstood principle. People often talk about how "stressed" they are. Or note that something is "stressing them out." They reference stress as something external that happens to them. This idea is not only false; it also leaves the person at the mercy of "stress."

Stress is an internal response to an external event. It can't be avoided entirely, but it can be managed well. Some people tend to fry themselves with stress— while others try to avoid "stress provoking situations" altogether. Both extremes can render us ineffective. There really is a happy, healthy medium.

For a moment, consider that events happening around us are neutral. The thoughts we have about them are what cause the stress. For example, one person can have five reports due at work and feel entirely stressed out. Another person can see those five same reports and feel excitement over the challenge. Same event. Different response. That is true with every external event.

Stress is internal, a way we are responding to those external events. It is really our interpretation of the external event. Speaking in public is a stress-out for some, exciting for others. Some relish competition. Others feel overwhelmed. External events are neutral. Your internal reaction—your thoughts and interpretation of that event, is the cause of the stress.

In truth, one of the ways we grow stronger is by dealing with challenges. For instance, when we stress a muscle with exercise, that muscle repairs itself and grows stronger. Then it can cope with more challenge.

Our life is the same way. As we learn to cope with the many stresses and challenges we face every day, we become more competent and confident—able to deal with whatever life throws our way with ever-greater skill, resilience, and equilibrium. This is particularly true when we utilize the tools we've been discussing while maintaining good boundaries that allow us to focus on what's really important to us.

Belly breathing is an excellent stress reliever. It's a wonderful way to tell your body that everything is okay. When we breathe with our chest, we are signaling to our brain that there is something to worry about. When we breathe with our belly, we indicate to our brain that it is safe to relax. Belly breathing is an excellent, natural way for defusing our instinctual fear reaction. As we breathe through our belly, our brain grows calm and our system relaxes.

Throughout the day, find some way of reminding yourself to breathe into your belly. Let the ringing of the phone or any other type of regular interruption be a signal to you to take a few deep breaths through your belly. Practicing this throughout the day will help calm your entire nervous system.

Also, take time to make sure that when you're involved in a lot of physical exertion, you take some time out for stress reduction. While the stress hormones that run through our body—including adrenaline and cortisol—are dissipated through movement, we also need intervals of relaxation. So, when you're feeling stressed out, move your body, breathe deeply through your belly, and you'll soon find yourself in a space of inner calm and greater relaxation. Then, it is easier to notice the thoughts running through your mind that are the true roots of your dis-stress.

Remember, as well, the other stress-reducing, calm-producing tools we've been discussing—like moments of gratitude and appreciation, the setting of clear boundaries, and the raising of your personal standards. Take time, as well, to focus on your purpose. All these things contribute to a less stressed, more productive, and enjoyable life.

☯ TL;DR—Care For Yourself ☯

- Part of thriving is taking care of your body, so that your body can take you into the world. When our bodies are neglected, our capacity of impacting ourselves (and the world) is diminished.

- Caring for yourself has nothing to do with external ideas of beauty or body, weight or shape. It is about making sure your body is functioning as well as it can, within the realm of the limitations you have. We all have various limitations.

- Focus on four areas of your health:

  1. Rest: Most research shows that most people need between 7 and 9 hours of quality sleep per night. If you get behind, you can't easily catch up. Establish a regular routine to help ensure your adequate rest.

  2. Exercise: Bodies are meant to move. But we live in a society that encourages sedentary lifestyles. Many people sit at desks all day. Moving is essential for the body. As is some exercise. Aim for 15 minutes of walking, or even a quick 7 Minute Workout throughout the week.

  3. Diet: Food is the fuel of the body. We tend to forget this and use food as a reward or punishment. Focusing on the best fuel for your body can be helpful. Aim for high qualities of protein, fat, and carbohydrates. Remember that calories are not equal. The net effect on your body is different, depending on the source of that calorie.

  4. Stress: Our bodies are not built for constant and chronic stress. Bodies are designed for acute stress, which passes and allows the body to return to a calm state. Stress, contrary to our automatic beliefs, is always an internal reaction to an external event. There is nothing inherently stressful about outward events, except for how we internally respond to them—and how we release those events after they pass.

Chapter 12

live your purpose

"Life is never made unbearable by circumstances, but only by lack of meaning and purpose."

—Viktor Frankl, M.D, Ph.D.

I t's kind of amazing—don't you think—that poets, philosophers, and scientists throughout the ages have all tried to discern the Purpose of Life. Yet, we still do not have one definitive answer with which everyone agrees.

On the one hand, this confirms that life is an unfathomable mystery that defies all attempts at explanation. On the other hand, it gives us a lot of latitude to just make it up as we go along—to find our own sense of purpose.

So what do you want the purpose of *your* life to be? That's the key question. And it's one that each of us has to decide for ourselves.

The 20th century American author and speaker on comparative mythology, Joseph Campbell, came to the conclusion that—"Life is without meaning."

That's a shocker, isn't it? He also said that it is up to each of us to ". . . bring the meaning to it."

Having studied how cultures around the world and throughout the ages have grappled with the question of life's meaning and purpose in their respective mythologies, Campbell saw that, "The meaning of life is whatever you ascribe it to be. Being alive is the meaning."

What it all seems to come down to, then, is this: How do you want to experience your own aliveness? And what can you do to feel more vitally alive?

For many people, it's living on the edge of life and death that heightens their awareness of their existence. That's why some people become risk takers. They derive pleasure from extreme sports in which they put their lives on the line each time they go out to "play." Other people become gamblers and put their fortune on the line when they play. And as soon as the thrill fades from whatever risky behavior they're involved in, both gamblers and athletes may opt to "raise the ante" in order to "push the envelope" and amp up their feeling of aliveness once again.

Many of the cancer patients I've counseled have also expressed a sense of heightened aliveness, precisely because they were facing their death. On such an edge, life becomes more precious and priorities become more clear. Roused from our routines, we recognize that life is so fragile and temporary. We also see that loving relationships have the most enduring value to us— above everything else.

So how can we have an awakened awareness of the value of life and the people we love—without having to risk our existence or our fortunes to obtain it? That's what Thrivers ask themselves repeatedly throughout their lives.

What's It All About?

For the vast majority of adults, I suspect, life can seem quite ordinary and even dull. We pretty much do the same things day after day, year after year. In fact, we could just about sleep walk through our routines and many people actually do that—even if they're not aware of it at the time. People move through, day after day, waiting for their real life to begin "when . . . ." The "when" can vary from person to person, but it is always beyond the current circumstances.

Instead of experiencing life as a precious gift, we tend to experience it as a humdrum routine of winning and losing—seeking pleasure and avoiding pain in all that we do. But then, how can we avoid the feeling of utter meaninglessness and the despair that comes with that?

One of the best people to answer that question is Dr. Viktor Frankl. An Austrian neurologist and psychiatrist, he was actually writing on that very subject when the Nazi's detained him and his family for being Jewish. Still, he continued to pursue his research and test his theories in the totally meaningless insanity of the Nazi death camps. There, he endured the murder of his wife and parents and observed the anguish that he and his fellow prisoners suffered moment-by-moment, day-after-day, year-after-year. This is what he concluded:

"Ultimately, man [sic] should not ask what the meaning of his life is, but rather must recognize that it is he who is asked. In a word, each man is questioned by life; and he can only answer to life by answering for his own life; to life he can only respond by being responsible."

According to Dr. Frankl, it is our ability to respond to life in accordance with our own values—and regardless of our circumstances—that is our purpose in life. And that purpose can save our lives—or, at least, make them more possible to endure intact when under great duress.

Dr. Frankl observed that a few of the prisoners in the camps went beyond their own pain and suffering to share what little food and comfort they had with others. And these were the ones who ended up faring the best. He concluded that, "The more one forgets himself—by giving himself to a cause to serve or another person to love—the more human he is and the more he actualizes himself."

What this says to me is that in order to thrive—in any situation—we need to bring forth our best Self. And the best way to do that is to live with a greater sense of Purpose, Meaning, and Value—in all of our relationships.

How Being of Service Brings Purpose

When we contribute to the lives of others, we contribute to our own sense of aliveness and personal value. Just think for a moment about what happens following a widespread disaster—when strangers who might not otherwise interact break out of their cages of propriety to rush to each other's aid.

The feelings of connection and compassion that persist in such extraordinary circumstances are akin to the good will we endeavor to muster around the Holidays. And we wish such feelings could last forever, because we feel more alive when we live from our hearts—and more on point when we're being of service to others, given how interconnected we all are. And this isn't just true of humans.

I am reminded of "working dog" breeds that often lose touch with the "working" part of their genes. These are dogs from breeds that have been bred for generations to fulfill vital roles on a ranch or farm—in partnership with their human "pack-leader." They're genetically programmed for work, but often have little opportunity to act on those tendencies.

I met a woman once who had an Australian Shepherd in Los Angeles. Like a doting mother taking a child to soccer practice, she would drive a great distance for her dog's weekly class in sheep herding. However, many people don't know how to provide their animal companion with the activity it needs to feel like it's fulfilling the purpose for which it was born.

One family I read about found a solution around this dilemma. They had their dog carry its food and water on its back in a little saddlebag. And this made a huge difference to its behavior. Evidently, it gave the dog the sense that it was serving an important role for the family. Now that it had a purpose to fulfill, the dog's mood and behavior settled down.

It may seem far-fetched that the problem with the dog was solved when it was given a job. But I've counseled a lot of suffering people who don't even recognize that a lack of meaning in their work and the absence of mutually beneficial connections with others were at the root of their unhappiness.

Humans (as well as other animals) are social beings. It is in our nature to play a role that contributes to the lives of those around us. Since even the smallest, seemingly insignificant life form in an eco-system makes an essential contribution to the well being of the entire system—imagine how essential it is to each one of us that we exercise our conscious capacity to make a positive difference in the lives of other beings. No one wants to feel that they don't matter.

Living in a Vacuum

We are meaning-creating beings. And without that sense of personal value that we contribute to the greater good, we tend to get into trouble because our lives feel disconnected from others and, thus, ultimately pointless.

A dog from a highly specialized working breed may go berserk in an urban environment until given a job to do. Similarly, a human being—disconnected from their purpose and "bliss"—lives an aimless existence. And this, I believe, is a condition that fuels addictions.

I've watched people try to lift their spirits with alcohol and fill the "hole in their Soul" with distractions of every description. Years can go by before the futility of their pursuits becomes fully apparent to them. That's often the time when they come to see me—to help them figure out why their life feels so flat and meaningless and how they can turn things around.

Actually, I believe a lack of deeper meaning in life is the basis for a mid-life crisis. At some point, all the adrenaline-producing pursuits of thrills, possessions, and experiences no longer work to numb the pain of a life that feels like it's going nowhere and serving no one.

The erratic behaviors we often see in a midlife crisis have a lot in common with an "unemployed" sheep dog living in a small apartment in New York. It's "crazy-making." People then go to extremes in an attempt to convince themselves that—"Hey, I'm alive!" Or they run around wondering, "Is this all there is? What am I missing? What's this whole thing about? How do I get to that place of feeling like who I am and what I do really matters?"

I'm convinced that only a sense of purpose—that involves using our gifts and interests in service to others—can save us from a life of meaninglessness and despair.

Follow Your Bliss (Sort of)

Many of us were raised with an ethic that said we must work hard and "do good" in order to be worthwhile. But is a life without joy worthwhile to us?

I think there's greater wisdom in the saying, "Do what you love and you'll never have to work a day in your life." When engaged, the sense of doing "work" falls away. So what is that you love to do?

If you don't know what that is right now, you might want to ask yourself some simple yet profound questions, like—"When do I feel most alive?" And "What do I most enjoy doing?" Or, "What did I love to do as a child—but then put aside for more practical pursuits?"

One of Joseph Campbell's most famous suggestions for finding your path and purpose in life is to "Follow your Bliss!" By doing so, you will ultimately find your aliveness, live a more meaningful existence, and be a more beneficial presence on the planet.

This quote by Campbell has often been misinterpreted. People started looking for something that enabled them to feel "bliss" all the time. Campbell's point was that when you pursue your bliss, you are willing to push through the struggles and challenges. In fact, when there is no struggle or challenge, whatever bliss we may experience is not likely to be sustainable or reliably repeatable. The challenge is part of the bliss.

To discover the kind of work that feels like play to us, we have to be willing to let go of what we think we *should* be doing, according to other people's beliefs and standards. Certainly, it's important to consider the opinion of wise and trusted advisors. But ultimately, I think one of the best pieces of advice on this subject comes from another 20th century luminary—the American author, activist, and theologian, Howard Thurman, who said: "Don't ask what the world needs, ask what makes you come alive and go do it. Because the world needs people who have come alive."

Not everybody is fortunate enough to make a living doing what they love. But some get so good at their quirky talents that they actually do. I just watched a YouTube video of the magician who won first place in *America's Got Talent*. He got turned on to magic at the age of four and over the years has developed capacities that stunned the judges and the entire audience. He followed his bliss and it led him to a fortune.

Of course, not everyone's favorite hobby earns them fame or fortune. Nevertheless, engaging in it regularly definitely lights up their lives. When we do whatever we do with love—*and* do what we love to do—we find that our lives grow ever more powerful and purposeful. We also find that we are filled with joy and gratitude as a natural consequence, regardless of circumstances.

Someone I know spent the majority of her working life at jobs that were of no interest to her. She was able to endure these menial jobs because she did what she loved each day before coming to work—and again when she got home, as well as all through the weekend. So, though her outer life was not much to her taste, her inner life grew ever more rich and rewarding. And now, her outer and inner lives are beginning to merge as her well-cultivated gifts have become of great value to others, as well.

Finding Our Purpose Right Where We Are

In another chapter I shared a story from my early career when I felt trapped in a dead end situation at a counseling center in the inner city. One day, I realized I had the option to quit or to suck it up and endure the seeming pointlessness of it all. I also saw that I might find a way to transform the situation.

That's what I chose to do. And that pursuit made a big, positive difference in my life as well as in the lives of the clients and counselors at the center. But let's face it: changing a dysfunctional system from the inside out, isn't always an option. Sometimes we really do just have to "suck it up."

I once counseled a client who owned a business pumping out septic tanks. "I don't like what I do," he told me. "It's not what I want to be doing. But it allows me to enjoy the rest of my life, doing what's meaningful to me." So he literally "sucked it up," made really good money in the process, then spent the rest of his time with his family, his hobbies, and his philanthropic pursuits.

I've also worked with clients who simply followed a well-worn path right into the family business. They grew up around doctors, dentists, investors, or attorneys, trained in the family profession, and then did what their relatives had been doing for years. At some point along the way, however, they woke up to the fact that they weren't really happy doing it. This path had no real meaning for them.

When someone realizes they've essentially been "sleep-walking" through their lives, then it really is time to make a shift. Sometimes, just a shift in location to a more harmonious environment is all that it takes for them to be able to derive meaning and value from the work they've been doing. But for others, only a shift in occupation can help them come awake and alive again.

The Lens Through Which We View the Lives We Lead

Sometimes, all it takes is a change in perspective to add meaning to one's work. For instance, I was working with a realtor once, who was doing really well at getting listings and selling houses. It's just that the work lacked real meaning for him. I asked him why this was so and he said, "Because what I'm doing is like playing a game of Monopoly—getting people in one house and out of another and then cashing the check."

So I asked him, "Did you ever think about the fact that what you're doing at a deeper level is helping people find a house and create a home?" He dismissed that idea. "Nah, I'm just buying and selling houses," he told me.

"That's one way to look at it," I said. "But here's another: At a pivotal moment in people's lives—when they're ready to move into a different home in which to experience the next phase of their life—you serve as their agent by helping them to find what they're seeking and at the very best price. That's a significant act of service that takes quite a bit of skill and experience, don't you think?" I asked him.

Seen in this light, my client changed his whole attitude about his work. He started finding meaning, value, and even pleasure in it. He was no longer viewing it as, "How can I get you into a house as fast as possible, make my money, and go on to the next client?" Instead, his inner dialogue became, "How can I create a win-win-win proposition that benefits the buyer, the seller, *and* me?" And that's all it took to turn an ordinary job into a greater purpose that gave meaning to his life—he was not a house-seller, but a home-finder. And by the way, it also increased his sales.

We sometimes have to take a closer look at the bigger picture to find value in what we're doing. But if our goal is to live a life of Purpose and Meaning, then we have the power to change our whole experience of what we're doing to make a living. And that can make an enormous difference in our sense of aliveness.

That's what happened for me at the counseling center where I had felt so trapped and ineffective—working with reluctant, delinquent youth who showed up under duress from the courts. I asked myself, "How can I make this more effective, meaningful, and enjoyable for everyone involved?" Finding a way to do that benefitted the youth, the counselors, and the whole community. That event changed the course of my life. I found that I could overcome my own discouragement and resistance by seeking a way to be of greater service to others. And in this way, I found meaning and purpose.

The Purpose Journey

We are created as a purpose builder, as a meaning maker. That is what humans are. When we don't do that, we're going to feel empty. And nothing from the outside can fill that emptiness up.

As I see it, purpose and meaning are very tightly interwoven. The high intentions we hold and the actions we take to fulfill them relate to the accomplishment of our Purpose. The value and deeper sense of aliveness we gain as a result of living purposeful lives is what we call Meaning. And when we feel that the work we do in the world is meaningful to others as well, we gain even more pleasure from it because then we are living for a purpose that is larger than just ourselves.

Challenges beset us all. Treasured people leave our lives. Fabulous careers come to an end. Dr. Frankl teaches us that we can find meaning in even the most meaningless of suffering by how we allow it to bring forth from within us greater resources of compassion and caring than we even knew we had. He wrote, "When we are no longer able to change a situation, we are challenged to change ourselves."

The purpose of our Life is to be our authentic selves ever more fully. And perhaps one of the greatest values we can gain from the endless challenges we face is our capacity to use them to transcend ourselves and to reveal the inner majesty we always knew was there.

TL;DR—Live Your Purpose

- The big question of life emerges: "What does it all mean and why am I here?" This is the question of meaning and purpose.
- While finding meaning is a philosophical question, approached from a multitude of directions, purpose is about action. "Purpose" is about finding meaningful action to take in the world.
- For most people, what gives a sense of purpose can shift over the course of a lifetime. The problem is when someone either loses or can't find a place of purpose. When purpose is lost, the temptation is to find momentary solace—leading to destructive actions, such as addiction.
- When people are focused on discovering and living out their life purpose, they begin to impact the world. That impact tends to grow, with ripples going out into the world. A place of purpose impacts the individual, their family, their friends, and eventually, the world.

Chapter 13

act on your convictions

"Your beliefs become your thoughts, your thoughts become your words, your words become your actions, your actions become your habits, your habits become your values, your values become your destiny."
—**Mahatma Gandhi**

a system of values is like the spine of a body: It must be strong enough to hold us upright throughout our life. It's meant to grow over time. And it has to stay flexible to enable us to maintain our youthful mobility. However, if it gets twisted in some way, it can throw us entirely out of alignment. And the pain and repercussions of that torque can last a lifetime.

Knowing what is truly meaningful to you—the values, traits, and qualities that you endeavor to cultivate in yourself and desire to see present in your family and friends—is the essential foundation and framework for a thriving life. Once your core values are in place, then they can serve as both a support and a compass to direct your whole life.

For instance, if your "True North" points toward loving kindness, then that will be the criteria by which you make decisions for your life. If your prime conviction is in the importance of "personal success at all costs," then your direction and choices in life will be quite different—as will be your results.

Theoretically, these two opposing choices could result in the accumulation of inner wealth for the first and outer wealth for the second. But as the lyric goes in a famous country-western song, "…the world's richest man is a pauper at times, compared to the man with a satisfied mind."

Ideally, of course we want it all—inner riches and outer wealth. But too often people are willing to sacrifice a piece of their own integrity for the material gain that such a "short-cut" can facilitate. Ironically, however, just as wealth cannot be fully enjoyed when health is compromised, so the "spoils of victory" can, over time, spoil our pleasure in what we've gained, if we did so at the cost of something truly valuable within us.

We've all heard of people who "have it all" yet still feel empty and needy inside. Because of a lack of awareness of the source of lasting happiness, the feeling of not *being* or *having* enough drives many to chase after more.

A Thriver, however, is someone who can experience great fullness with or without great wealth or possessions. When they stay true to their convictions of what is truly of value to them in life, and strive to meet their own standards for how they want to show up in the world, they experience a wealth of being that money cannot buy.

Convictions and their Repercussions

Life is a series of choices. And every choice we make contributes to the quality of the person we are and are becoming. When we are presented with options—and base our choice on what we think other people will think about us—then we don't get the chance to fully develop into our best Self under all circumstances. But when we aim high—and seek to continually elevate the quality of person we are—then the choices we make may also inspire others to live their greater truth in the world.

Think back to a time when you made a decision based on some deeper conviction of what was right for you to do in that instance. And you acted on your decision, in spite of what was going on around you. Maybe your friends were encouraging you to take the easy road. Or it might have been a voice inside your own head that said, "C'mon. It's not that big a deal. No one has to know and no one will get hurt. Just look at how this one little crossing of the line could really help me get to where I've been wanting to go for so long."

Despite the seductive outer and inner persuasion, you still knew that—small as it might seem—crossing the line wasn't really the right thing to do. So, you didn't do it. You lost out on a "sweet deal," and perhaps on the winking approval of your friends. And that didn't feel so good. But what you ultimately got instead was a really sweet, clean feeling inside yourself—along with greater trust and reliance on the strength of your spine of ethical convictions.

Now, compare that feeling to the one you had when you *did* succumb to pressure or to the temptation of the pay-off that was available—just by cutting one little ethical corner or two. You got the prize you were after, but it may not have felt so good on the back end. Of course, that unpleasant feeling of having compromised yourself may have faded over time. But it could well linger longer as a subtle undertone that undermines your self-esteem.

When Thrivers use their convictions as their GPS, or moral compass, they are able to navigate the sometimes tight and twisty passages between ethically ambiguous situations. They value that sweet, clean feeling that comes from playing things straight. And they aren't willing to trade that in for some temporary advantage. Thus, they are creative in life. They are led by their positive aspirations, rather than reacting out of fear or in pursuit of a temporary advantage that comes at the cost of small compromises in their values along the way.

Conviction in Oneself

There's really only one person's trust we ever have to win and maintain—and that's our own. In order to feel safe and stable inside, we need to know that we can count on our self to live in accordance with our own convictions. If we do what we know is right on one occasion, but then fudge it a bit on the next, we create a place of uncertainty within ourselves.

Given the degree of instability in the outer world, it really helps to feel that our internal guidance system—our conviction in and dedication to the values by which we live our life—can help us stay in balance and on-track no matter how topsy-turvy our world may become. When we act on our own convictions, our experience of the world becomes a bit more stable.

Our intention to live by our convictions—when no one is looking, or when everyone is looking—gives us a quiet inner strength that other people can sense. If we uphold our convictions both in private and in public, then we develop true self-reliance. Other people's opinions no longer exert a strong influence on us, especially if they're not in keeping with our convictions. That's a beautiful ideal and something we can grow into choice-by-choice-by-choice.

Convictions are based on our aspirations—for the kind of person we wish to become and how we want to move through the world. When we understand what we want, elevate our standards as we go, set clear workable boundaries, take responsibility for our lives, and recognize that our thoughts have only the power we give them with our intentions and attention, then we're better able to act in accordance with our convictions, rather than our momentary convenience.

Going back to the analogy of our core values as our spine, we can see how we build the muscles that support our spine every time we act in accordance with our personal values.

Then, something else quite interesting occurs. Our fidelity to our values actually creates a magnetic resonance that forms a boundary of sorts within and around us. And this boundary instantly alerts us with feelings of discomfort whenever we transgress it. An error in judgment that puts us in an uncomfortable position may feel as if we are wearing our left shoe on our right foot.

I Cannot Tell a Lie (Or Accept A Lie)

A woman I know who worked as a secretary in business offices for many years, thought nothing of helping herself to office supplies in support of activities she performed at night for a world peace organization. It took some time before it dawned on her that what she was doing—though certainly "for a good Cause"—was essentially stealing. At some point, she recognized her petty theft was actually a contradiction to the very cause for which she was acting in this unethical manner. She understood then that the Ends do not justify the Means. And she immediately made amends and cleaned up her act.

Over time, honesty and integrity became so important to her that she wouldn't dream of acting unfairly. She never takes advantage of a cashier's oversight in giving her too much money in change. She also finds it impossible to be dishonest without extreme discomfort—so she avoids situations that would require more self-disclosure than feels appropriate to her.

This woman shifted from a place of thoughtlessly acting against her convictions to moving toward and into these convictions as her way of life. She gave up the "What can I get?" mentality that often pulls us off course and shifted to "What is congruent with my convictions?"

Some time later, this same woman met a much younger man who wrote beautiful poetry. They spoke on several occasions and enjoyed sharing their creative writing with each other. He expressed great admiration for her work and purported to be a close friend of a famous actor who owned a publishing company. He was sure that the woman's work would be a perfect fit for that company and offered to introduce her to the actor when he came into town late the following week. The woman looked up the publishing house on-line, saw the potential fit for her work, and was delighted with the possibility.

Over the intervening weekend, she went to lunch with a group of friends at a local restaurant. At some point in the course of their meal one woman glanced at a nearby table and said to the others, "Isn't that X?"—the very actor who was supposedly out of town for another five days.

The woman in our story excused herself and went over to introduce herself to the actor as a friend of the fellow that supposedly knew him well. "Who?," the actor inquired of her. She repeated the name of the young man who was going to introduce them. "Never heard of him," the actor said, shaking his head and returning to his lunch.

She apologized for the intrusion and returned to her table of friends a bit stunned and confused. Apparently, the young man who wrote such lovely poetry and offered to be her liaison with a publisher—was a total fraud.

The woman wondered how this could have happened. The quality of people who came into her life had elevated over the years in parallel with her own ethical conduct. Given her efforts to live out her convictions, she had raised her standards and her boundaries. And those around her had, not coincidentally, also been of higher standards.

This doesn't mean that the woman now feels safe to forego all precautions with the people she allows into her life. Not at all! But she does operate with a high level of trust that the atmosphere of integrity she's created within herself will be mirrored by the people she encounters in the outer world. And thus far, her trust has been borne out.

As for the man who got through her "barrier," he called the following Monday to set up a meeting with the actor for her. "He's coming into town tomorrow," he said. "And I'll be seeing him on Wednesday. So plan on Thursday or Friday for a meeting."

Knowing his deception had to have been the product of his insecurity, the woman kindly told him of her experience at the restaurant. And she asked him why he thought he needed to impress her—and why he had resorted to a lie in an effort to do so.

In the few minutes of their brief phone conversation, he was at first silent, then dishonest, then confessed. Then, he disappeared from her life. She thought of how sad and ironic it was that this strong young man—who was a body builder and a martial artist (as well as a poet)—had such an ethical weakness because of his hunger to win other people's esteem and approval. Those tend to be the very issues that pull people away from their convictions.

Why We May Forsake Ourselves

Let's face it: the desire to be accepted by others and the fear of their negative opinions about us can motivate us to act in ways that are incongruent with our deeper values. As young children, we want to please our parents. And if they withheld their love and approval from us, we were likely to go to great lengths—even to self-betrayal—in order to win it from them.

As adults, it can be very challenging to feel worthwhile—and to take full responsibility for our own actions—if we didn't get a good start in life and don't really like whom we perceive that we are. And it's so much easier to blame a person or a situation as the cause of our ethical lapses. By so doing, we may grant ourselves some latitude—at least in our own mind—for making choices that forsake our own convictions. But, over time, the inner "muscles" that support our spine of values weaken. And little by little, small compromises add up to major distortions in the posture we hold in the world.

Acquiescing in favor of "Group Think" can be a strong pull for people with a shaky sense of their own value and a great need to be part of a community. Of course, there are also those people who seem to operate exclusively from self-interest and without concern for their impact on others. Whatever the cause, they hold an ethic that puts personal success above everyone and everything else. Clearly, their conscience and awakened awareness of connection with others are not in good working order.

In order to thrive, we cannot act like chameleons of other individuals and groups. We are called upon to stand on our own convictions in the face of whatever pressures we may feel inside us or that others may exert upon us. We may suffer their disapproval in the short-term. But by being true to ourselves, we avoid the more damaging consequences that come with self-compromise.

Fortunately, wherever we are on the spectrum of self-esteem and in the practice of thriving habits, we can always get better. By discovering the values that truly resonate with our hearts and minds, and taking small steps every day to live in accordance with these values, we gain greater inner strength and confidence. We also develop a thriving attitude toward life that allows us to live with greater autonomy, dignity, compassion, and joy.

Also important, and a fortunate side-effect, is that by continually making ethical choices with the "Highest Good of All" in mind, we are actually less prone over time to attract people into our lives who operate at a lower ethical standard. And if we maintain a "growth attitude" throughout our lives, in which we seek to learn from every situation we encounter, then if or when we do interact with someone with questionable values, we find ways of turning the problems that may ensue into stepping-stones to higher learning, deeper wisdom, and greater value.

Acting on Conviction

Our spine of values is meant to grow with us. Like the woman in the office who was freely helping herself to supplies, we may have habitual, reactive patterns and behaviors in which we do what we've always done, without thinking of the larger implications. Until we wake up. Then, more and more, we determine our actions by how they resonate inside us, rather than by what we can gain outwardly from them. And these become the rules we live by.

A therapist with the given name of Merlin used to say to his clients, "When you do what's right for you, it's right for everyone!" That's a powerful recognition that by keeping our "spine" of values healthy—through exercising choices that support our core values—we actually benefit everyone around us, whether we can see it and they know it or not. When we consider the short *and* long-term impact of our choices on other people, it helps us stay true to ourselves.

The very young son of a friend of mine was struck by his easy access to tempting items at an outside market, and how readily he could take something he wanted without getting caught. My friend agreed that it would be very easy to take it when no one was looking. But she told him that there would always be one witness he could never escape. He thought she meant herself, his mom, and she could almost see the wheels turning in his head. So, she quickly explained to him that the set of eyes that were always on him were his own.

She explained that when we act in a way that we know is unfair or unkind to another, the good feelings we may have about what we gain would eventually be replaced by remorse and probably guilt. Doing what we know is right, even when no one is looking, is a gift we give to ourselves that "works for everyone." It's what allows a community of people to function together with freedom, trust, and honor.

Acting on our convictions may sometimes stand in the way of achieving our immediate desired outcomes. But when we live by what feels right, rather than what may feel good in the moment, we build an inner strength and wealth that brings enduring value to our life. We may also achieve outer prosperity—but we refuse to sell our integrity for it.

Thrivers think about the end result, and how they will feel down the line, before making a decision—large or small. That's a standard that helps Thrivers act on conviction more often than not.

Thrivers understand the importance of choosing their actions based on their moral compass. They know that their task is to become more and more responsible for their own lives. They recognize that by raising and then reaching their standards throughout their lives, they actually elevate their life condition. And they accept that it's each person's job to do this for him or her self—rather than to impose a way of life on others who may see life differently.

This doesn't mean that Thrivers are free of temptation or immune to the allure of easy gain. None of us are. But as they say in 12-Step Programs, healing is about progress not perfection.

The truer we are to our personal convictions, the more integrated they become into our unconscious operating system. Being kind and ethical becomes our "default setting," regardless of whether anyone's watching or whatever anyone else is doing.

Convictions vs. Certainty

It's very important that the values we choose to live by are positive ones, representing what we intend to stand for in our life—and not what we stand against. Against-ness may temporarily benefit from the fiery energy of anger and adrenaline. But ultimately, it burns us out. Support for what we believe in keeps us strong throughout our lives—but only if we allow our spine of values to grow by keeping our minds open to new information and by sharpening our discernment.

There's a high probability that though we may have total conviction in the correctness of our values and opinions, we could one day have an awakening experience that dramatically alters our perspective. As the author David Foster Wallace said in a 2005 university commencement address, "Blind certainty [is] a close-mindedness that amounts to an imprisonment so total that the prisoner doesn't even know he's locked up."

Here's an illustration of that point: A filmmaker from Iran made a documentary (*Bam 6.6*) about a young Jewish couple that loved trekking the world together. In 2003 they went to Bam, Iran, where he intended to ask her to marry him. The day before that big event, a far bigger one occurred: A magnitude 6.6 earthquake struck as they slept and both were buried under rubble. He was among the nearly 28,000 people killed by the quake. She was one of over 30,000 who survived.

When her parents came from the U.S. to be with her, they were met at the plane with flowers and a driver to take them to the hospital. Her father profusely thanked the surgeon for saving his daughter's life and asked what he owed him—monetarily speaking. "Nothing," the surgeon replied. "She is a guest in our country. It is my responsibility to help her."

The young woman's mother, a registered nurse, commented in the documentary on the astounding level of care and compassion her daughter received from the nurses and other medical staff as she recovered from her injuries. She'd never seen anything like it in any hospital in which she'd ever practiced nursing in the United States.

I share this story primarily because of a certified letter the filmmaker received from someone who said he'd been "forced" to watch the film. The man wrote that he had very fixed opinions about Iran and its people. He'd formed such "certainties" through his unquestioning acceptance of what was conveyed repeatedly by the media in the U.S.

In the letter, he spoke of his great shame and remorse for holding such a hostile, aggressive, and condemning attitude toward the people of Iran. He could not get over how close-minded and prejudiced he'd been. He simply thought that he was standing on principle against an evil nation of people that operated with ill intent toward the United States.

Along with his statement of remorse he enclosed a check for $250— knowing that the filmmaker had mortgaged his home and maxed-out his credit cards to make this beautiful, impactful documentary that had totally shifted his "certainties" and opened him up to his own heart of compassion.

Staying True to Oneself

The filmmaker clearly lived up to his own convictions through his efforts to promote understanding and peace between his country and the United States. He did so at great personal risk, by investing so much time, effort, and expense to make the film—while knowing that only *after* they saw his final cut would the parents of the couple at the heart of the film give their approval and permission for him to show it.

The letter writer had also been living in accordance with his principles and convictions—by acting with prejudice and hostility toward people he'd never met from a nation he'd been taught to fear and despise. This underscores the point about the importance of standing *for* something and not *against* something else.

We may feel charged with adrenaline, which serves to reinforce our sense of moral rectitude when we take a negative stance. But then, our actions may move us in a direction that actually undermines what we truly hold as a core value. To keep our behavior aligned with our values, we need to remain open to new information, as the letter writer (reluctantly) proved himself to be.

David Foster Wallace, in the same commencement address, said that truly learning to think required him, "To be just a little less arrogant. To have just a little critical awareness about myself and my certainties. Because a huge percentage of the stuff that I tend to be automatically certain of is, it turns out, totally wrong and deluded."

Compassionate acceptance of our own, and other people's, choices and lifestyles is the hallmark of a thriving person. It actually keeps us healthy and focused on our own development. Judgment, on the other hand, reduces our worldview and our capacity to connect.

Can you imagine what life would be like in the U.S. if the majority of members of Congress knew this? Each side seems to possess the certainty that they are correct and the other side corrupt. And such certainty and "against-ness" only amplifies animosities and slows down the evolution of the entire society. Clearly, the country is not thriving—and it likely won't until more individuals commit themselves to doing what it takes to thrive.

Life Puts Us to the Test

A friend of mine describes how, shortly after Nelson Mandela was released from prison and elected president of South Africa, she saw news coverage of a meeting he had with President Bill Clinton. As the two heads of state descended the steps of the capitol building, Clinton stumbled and the much older Mandela rushed to steady him on his feet. In her eyes, Clinton looked like a "lightweight" next to the elder statesman.

The 19th Century theologian James Freeman Clarke captured the contrast she perceived between the two men when he wrote, "The difference between a politician and a statesman is that a politician thinks about the next election while the statesman thinks about the next generation."

She thought of how Mandela's strength and uprightness were forged in the cauldron of a grueling and abusive 27-year stint in prison. As accurately portrayed in the biopic *Invictus*, Mandela would recite to himself the poem by that name whenever his courage was flagging and his will to keep going—with no hope in sight—needed some serious reinforcement.

Here are the last six lines of that famous poem written by the influential Victorian poet, William Ernest Henry:

> . . . *the menace of the years*
> *Finds, and shall find, me unafraid.*
> *It matters not how strait the gate,*
> *How charged with punishments the scroll.*
> *I am the master of my fate:*
> *I am the captain of my soul.*

As Mandela so poignantly demonstrated, holding on to our core values, even under extreme pressure, can transform an ordinary person into someone strong enough to change the course of history and move an entire nation in a positive direction.

Few of us are ever called upon to undergo such a rigorous challenge, or to stake our whole life on our core values. But all of us are forged by the succession of choices and challenges we face each day.

By holding firm to our convictions—and refusing to compromise our integrity under any circumstance—we, too, develop dignity and stature instead of pride and rigidity. And we, too, can make a positive difference in the lives of the people around us.

As Winston Churchill advised, "Never give in—never, never, never, never, in nothing great or small, large or petty, never give in except to convictions of honour and good sense." To that we might add—always stay open to having our conviction evolve when presented with new information. By such means Thrivers gradually but steadily elevate their life condition such that eventually they may stand out in a crowd—as exemplars of excellence—without even speaking a word.

TL;DR—Act On Your Convictions

- Your own values and convictions keep you strong and upright through life. They guide your choices and directions in life—as long as you keep them in focus.
- Sometimes, acting on convictions is about what you choose when nobody is looking. And sometimes, it is about what you choose when everyone is watching.
- As we raise our own personal standards, our convictions gain strength. The more we honor our convictions, the easier it is to raise our standards. They go hand-in-hand.
- Acting on convictions is not about acting against someone else. It is acting in the direction of your own values. Staying true to yourself is not ever against someone or something else.

Chapter 14

be courageous

"Courage is the mother of all virtues because without it, you cannot consistently perform the others."
—Aristotle

i t takes courage and determination to be oneself and to thrive in this world when so much in society seems dead set against it. We are bombarded all day, every day, by media that uses sophisticated marketing strategies and advances in neuroscience to make us believe we're dependent on sources outside ourselves for almost everything we need to live a happy, successful, and thriving life.

The news, entertainment, and advertising industries all endeavor to instill in us fear, and the desire for an endless array of costly "non-necessities." They then solve our "problems" with their products and services to satisfy these manufactured desires—along with strategies to protect us from false threats to our safety, self-esteem, and sense of well-being.

In such an atmosphere it's easy to forget that we have the capacity to thrive no matter what! But what does it take to counter the powerful gravitational pull of stories and images that push us toward our basest nature and our most persistent fears?

In the preceding chapters, we've touched upon perspectives and practices we can employ to counter forces in the world that seek to undermine our innate capacity to be awake and aware and to take full responsibility for our lives. These include:

- The recognition that a thought is just a thought and that we don't have to allow our momentary state of mind to dictate our choices and behaviors;
- The acceptance of "the things we cannot change" rather than the wasting of energy trying to fight against them;
- Forgiving of self and others to release the old hurts that hold us back;
- Showing up fully in our lives and being present to what's going on in the moment;
- Experiencing gratitude for the abundance we enjoy *and* for the challenges that can educate and strengthen us if we use them in that way;
- Developing our own conscious connection to what is bigger than us— that deeper presence in the world and at the heart of every being;
- Creating and communicating boundaries related to how we expect to be treated by others;
- Establishing and living by our own high standards and values;
- Taking care of the body, so we can function optimally in the world;
- Connecting with our sense of purpose—our reason for being—which makes it easier to persevere as we face the inevitable obstacles along the way; and
- Living in accordance with our convictions—rather than compromising them for easy gain.

In the next chapter, we will consider our capacity—and the profound necessity—to make a positive impact on the world. And then, we will explore how all of these practices support our personal growth and the actualization of our greater potential.

In this chapter, we will look at the quality of courage—in the face of fear—required to move out of our Comfort Zone and into the Impact Zone. This is the place we need to be, if we are to affect positive change in our own lives and in the world around us. But to understand courage, we first have to understand fear—so we know what we're up against and how to move beyond it.

I've noticed that courage is one of those misunderstood ideas. Years ago, my son was a Cub Scout, and I was assisting in leading those boys. We were involved in an art project, and I heard the boys talking about an incident that had happened. They were discussing the courage of the "hero" of this story.

I had to ask, "Guys, what does it mean to be courageous?" The table of boys all earnestly told me that courage was not having fear. I pondered that for a moment.

Then I suggested, "If you have no fear and you do something, you are just doing something. If you are being courageous, you are doing something in spite of the fear. Courage isn't about having no fear, it is choosing to act anyway, IN SPITE OF the fear."

How Fear Keeps Us Small

Courage is not the absence of fear but the willingness to move forward in the face of fear. Sometimes, in situations where an instantaneous response is required, a sudden surge of adrenaline may be triggered by the fear, allowing a person to perform some extraordinary feat in the moment. And often, afterwards, the person who acted with such courage will be as astounded as any spectator at the greater force that seemed to take them over and to use them for this heroic act. It seemed to be automatic

But consciously throwing our lives into what feels like danger requires that we override our own hard wiring, since our brain's first and foremost instinct is to keep us (or loved ones) safe. Whenever we feel unsafe, an alarm goes off—triggering the "fight, flight, or freeze" response. However, as is often pointed out, our brain evolved to protect us from threats in a radically different environment than we live in today.

As we discussed in an earlier chapter, our ancient ancestors faced life-and-death struggles moment-by-moment from the elements, the terrain, and the enormous animal predators with whom they shared caves and bushes, jungles, and savannahs. The ones who were the most vigilant in the face of all of these imminent dangers survived and passed their DNA on to us. In other words, the most fearful survived. Now, as their genetic heirs, we frequently have to deal with our fear-based projections and pessimistic tendencies in a relatively benign environment. In other words, we are overly wired for fear.

Our mind is programmed to look for trouble and to keep us safe. Picture a dog relentlessly sniffing around for a bone to pick, and you'll get the picture of how it is for most people. We are constantly sniffing out something to fear. And if we allow our mind to operate without our conscious supervision, it will dig up all sorts of dirt and have us in a state of perpetual emotional turmoil.

Letting our mind tell us what to think and do is like letting our dog take us out for a walk—which many people do. Unless we exert our authority, we'll be constantly tugged at the end of the "leash" such that we end up spending too much time in a fearful place and not nearly enough in our aspirational space.

Have you heard the saying, "The mind is a wonderful tool but a terrible master"? The transformational teacher, Byron Katie, made a startling discovery one day in a halfway house that changed her life. And it has helped change the lives of thousands of people around the globe to whom she has taught her process for questioning the mind.

Katie says,

"I discovered that when I believed my thoughts, I suffered, but that when I didn't believe them, I didn't suffer, and that this is true for every human being. Freedom is as simple as that. I found that suffering is optional. I found a joy within me that has never disappeared, not for a single moment."

A thriving life requires courage—which often involves reclaiming our minds and questioning our fears. If, instead, we allow ourselves to be led by our mind, we'll never get where we want to go. Or, even if we do get there—we won't be able to thrive once we've arrived. The encroaching fears will just pull us back down.

F.E.A.R.

Though the threats to our existence are so different today than they were for early humans, we still operate with the same amped-up survival system. This can cause us to feel paralyzed by fear and unable to take the necessary "risks" that would allow us to fulfill our dreams. The fear of public speaking is an excellent example. It has been reported that for many people, it's right up there alongside death as one of the most feared things in life.

Most of the fears that hold us back today exist primarily in our imagination. And the more attention we pay to these fears (which are really just thoughts)— and the more credence we give the beliefs (also just thoughts) that empower them—the larger they grow in our minds and the smaller we consequently feel. We can either empower ourselves (by noting these are just thoughts) or empower our fears (by believing those thoughts).

We can't move forward and claim a greater piece of life if we're always listening to the voice of fear within us. This doesn't mean we have to disregard our own (real) safety. But when fear intervenes to prevent our greater expression, then it is the fear, itself, that is a threat to our well-being and an impediment to thriving.

Fears are not to be ignored. There are times when the danger is real. There are times when something has truly put us at risk. To pretend otherwise is to place one's self at risk. But other times, those fears are not about true threats, but perceived or pretended threats. For example, there is little chance that speaking in public is going to do us bodily harm (barring a tomato thrown our way). This is more of a created fear, based in thoughts.

Chances are, you've seen the word "fear" presented as an acronym: *False Evidence Appearing Real*. Being able to distinguish the true from the false is essential for living courageously and moving effectively throughout our life journey.

Fear will always be with us, in part because it protects us from real risks and in part because it is the same energy as excitement. Learning how to discern the difference between fear and excitement—and how to respond appropriately to our feelings in the moment—are essential keys for thriving in the world.

Avoidance or Importance?

Though fear kept our ancient forbearers safe, today it keeps us small if we look upon our fear as a valid indication that danger is lurking. That's why it's so important not to "buy into" fear every time it arises in our awareness. Although we have an automatic reaction to fear, we can learn to consciously respond to it with greater discernment. After all, sometimes fear is a signal from our body that something important and unusual is occurring. So, either it's important that we get out of the way of danger—or important that we get out of our *own* way.

Imagine you're going on a job interview and it's a job you don't really want. Chances are, you don't have much anxiety or fear around it. So, you walk into the office with no built-up tension or fear because you don't attach much importance to what's about to happen. You know that if you don't get this job, another one will come along that you might like even better.

Now, think about that dream job you've been wanting for so long. Suddenly, it opens up and you've been asked to come in for a job interview. You're overwhelmed with excitement—or is it fear? Should you run from it—or to it? You feel like doing both at the same time.

This is an example of how the same physical sensations in the body can be interpreted very differently. And depending on what we call it—fear or excitement—our response to these sensations will also be very different. That's why discernment and self-management are so helpful at a time like this.

Now imagine you're a single person at a party. You meet a pleasant person and have a fun conversation. You are easy going, witty, and relaxed because you have no investment in the outcome. Then, you see someone across the room that looks to be your ideal partner. Suddenly, your heart is pounding and your palms are getting sweaty. You feel a knot in your stomach. Your breath is short and all your senses are on high alert. You want to go over there and start a conversation but a chorus of "What If's...." assail your mind and hold you back from taking that first step. Or, perhaps you go over there, trying to sound suave and cool—only to trip on your tongue or shoelace. You are a bundle of nerves because the importance you've ascribed to this meeting is way too high.

In these examples—of a dream job or of seeing someone who looks like your "ideal" partner—if we allow the fear to dictate our behavior, we end up staying safe but sorry. We cannot help but feel disappointed in ourself and in our life. We're playing too small to make enough room for our dreams and thus our happiness.

Have you ever wondered how people involved with extreme sports—or extreme negotiations—do it? I've had the opportunity to ask. And what I've discovered is that they have the same fears as the rest of us and experience the same weird sensations in their bodies. They just interpret them differently.

They recognize these feelings as excitement—mixed with fear—and use them as a way of staying focused and making sure they're taking all the necessary safety precautions. If they're base jumping, they're carefully folding up their parachutes, because they know their life depends on it.

Extreme athletes use their fear as an important indicator of potential danger. They know they're taking a calculated risk and that they have to be extremely careful. While spectators may believe that they have no fear at all, the truth is that they're just using their fear very differently than most of the rest of us do.

Our culture seems to use fear as something to avoid, an *Avoidance Indicator*, if you will. We interpret something as fearful, and thus to be avoided. I asked a client today, "Why didn't you give it a try?" to one of my suggestions from the prior week. He told me, "Because it scared me." Fear blocked him. He avoided.

In reality, fear should be seen as an *Importance Indicator*. The feeling of fear is definitely telling you something. But it isn't necessarily saying, "This is unsafe. Stay away from it." It could be indicating that, "This is important. Take note." That job you always wanted? Your fear was telling you how important it was. That person across the room? Your fear was telling you how important that relationship might be.

This is true for real dangers, too. When I am running on the trails in the woods, if I see something squiggly on the trail, it is important to pay attention. I might need to avoid the snake. It is important to my safety for me to avoid it!

Real fears *and* perceived fears are *Importance Indicators*. Your mind and body are screaming, "Pay attention! This is important!" Don't interpret it as "Avoid at all costs." Opportunities are missed when fear is used for avoidance.

Courage comes from paying attention and choosing your path.

Existential Fear

There's a whole other level of fear that underlies so much of our behavior—whether we know it or not. I refer to it as existential fear because it relates to anxieties that most, if not all, of us hold about our very existence, often just below our conscious awareness. And such fears make it harder to show up with courage in life.

Existential fears can wake us up at 3 a.m. and cause us to feel cold, frightened, and alone. Fears of this nature revolve around three primary issues: The fear that we won't have enough; the fear that we're not good enough; and the fear that we won't be loved enough.

1. The fear of not having enough is one of the most basic fears and it affects almost everyone—regardless of how much someone may actually possess. In fact, many people who experience the greatest tug from this fear are those who have more than enough. But the needle keeps moving up. What is "enough" is always just beyond what is.

Feeling that we don't have enough (money, friends, time, toys, health, or whatever) can lead to dysfunctional behaviors like hoarding, in which a person's home may get stacked from floor to ceiling with all manner of junk and trash. But hoarding is actually built into our genes.

This is true, even on a cellular level. Humans have lived through times of feast and times of famine. And it was those who were most efficient at holding onto those extra calories that got to pass their genes on to us. The people who burned calories fast were more likely to perish in times of famine. That's why our bodies are predisposed at a cellular level to hold on to more than they need. For the vast majority of us, it is far easier to gain weight than it is to lose it.

The existential fear of not having enough compels many people to do more in order to earn more so they can have more—and maybe feel like they *are* more as a result. Yet, few people arrive at the end of their lives regretting the time they took away from work to enjoy themselves and their family. They see, instead—though often not until the last moments—that they spent way too much time at the office for fear of not having enough.

A corporation's bottom line benefits greatly from all the efforts extended by people who are driven by fear to work harder, longer hours. However, the reward for the diligent worker is often only more responsibility, more stress, and more time away from the family. The cost of doing more to have more can take a very heavy toll on people's relationships, health, and well-being. And "enough" always remains just out of reach.

Our bodies are designed to live with stress for short periods of time but not for entire careers. In the short term, stress creates a readiness in the body for that fight-or-flight response. In the long term, our bodies begin to break down when exposed to a constant level of stress, which contributes to adrenal burnout, high blood pressure, diabetes, and even cancer.

To be clear, there is a need to have enough. We all need enough food to nourish our bodies and enough resources to be comfortable. The *fear* of not having enough has nothing to do with having enough. It is a fear that can exist in the imagination, even when there is more than enough.

2. The fear of not being good enough nips at all our heels. We tend to judge ourselves by unrealistic standards, often based on comparing what we know of our own weaknesses to what we perceive as someone else's strengths. As is said in 12-step programs, we are comparing our "insides" with someone else's "outsides," our sense of a flawed self with another person's appearance of strength and invulnerability. We cannot possibly end up feeling anything other than deficient when we make those comparisons. And we cannot thrive when we let the fear of not being good enough run our life.

As with all fears, it is not about being good enough, but the fear of not being good enough. The desire to improve is an excellent trait. It leads to growth and development (we will look at that shortly). But the fear of not being good enough tends to shut us down, not drive us forward. Being better, learning more, and moving forward, always moves us toward thriving. Fearing we are not good enough just keeps us stuck.

Our fear of not being good enough, in evolutionary terms, relates to the survival of the fittest. The fear is that if we're not good enough, we will not get the resources we need to pass our genes on to the next generation. And this brings up the third existential fear.

3. The fear of not being loved enough relates to how important connection with a community is to our survival, as well as to our sense of "okayness." Studies show that when people do not experience enough affection and love as infants and children, their long-term development is negatively impacted.

For adults, one of the highest-ranking determinants of life satisfaction is having loving relationships. Friends and family may fulfill that role for us. But often, we also want to experience an extended web of caring connections, so we participate with other close communities—like special interest clubs, churches, social organizations, etc.

To experience oneself as an acceptable and integral part of any social group can both save and threaten our lives. Young people raised without loving, supportive families may seek membership in violent gangs just to feel they have a place in "society" where they belong. And many people remain in dysfunctional relationships for the very same reason.

The fear of not being loved enough is what has us worried about our relationships, our romantic lives, and what other people think of us—including total strangers. It can influence how we interact with other people. It can also affect how far we are willing to go outside our own integrity to avoid being rejected.

Some people avoid connections with others because they're afraid of losing whatever acceptance and affection they may temporarily gain. Given these challenges, which all of us of face to one degree or another, we act courageously every single day when we endeavor to go beyond them.

Be All You Can BE

I believe we all share the desire to stand tall in our lives and to transcend the little self. We are aware that there is so much more to us—and within us—than we're called upon to use under ordinary circumstances. We all have the desire to rise up, to be the best we can be.

With this in mind, the army has used the slogan, "Be All You Can Be," as a way to attract young people to the military. The inference is that the training the military will provide—and the challenges that soldiers will be compelled to face—will serve as catalysts for self-actualization and heroism.

During the Viet Nam War in the mid-sixties, the Pulitzer-Prize winning author, Professor Ernest Becker, pointed out to his protesting students at UC Berkeley that the reason some young men were attracted to war was because it was the last "theatre of self-transcendence" left in the culture. When and where in normal civilian life does someone have the opportunity to rise up with courage and make a difference for others?

Many indigenous cultures hold initiation rites for young men and women to mark their passage into adulthood. In some cultures, such rites require enormous physical and emotional endurance and may precipitate some surprising results.

In the Western world, there are few if any challenging rites-of-passage to mark and precipitate the transition from childhood into young adulthood. There is the Quinceañera—celebrating the 15th birthday of young women—in Latin American communities. And there are Bar- and Bat-Mitzvahs for 13th year old sons and daughters in Jewish communities.

Fraternities and sororities—as well as street gangs—have initiatory rites of passage to welcome new members to the tribe and to put them to the test. But for the most part, no such recognition occurs within the community when a person leaves childhood behind. There are no real opportunities for a young person to have a sense of stepping into something greater than what was—except maybe that they can now go into a bar and drink.

The Men's movement, which began in the 1960's and 70's in response to the Women's Movement, sought to redress this lack of ritual—and to address the need all people have to be welcomed and embraced by an accepting community and encouraged to become more than they currently are. Most of us, however, go through life without any rite of passage—and without much sense of belonging. This lack in our life makes courage even harder to call forth, since courage, at its root, is a quality of heart.

Leaps of Faith and Courage

Acts of courage are actually acts of self-transcendence in which we go beyond what we normally desire to do or even feel that we can do.

If we don't take that leap when called upon to do so, we may fall into self-contempt. But when—in that crucial instant—we do go for it, we may catapult ourselves into a whole new level of self-perception and expression.

In a leap of faith—which sometimes happens spontaneously before we can even think about it—our survival instinct takes a back seat to our will to go beyond our limitations, possibly in service to another. Once we come down to Earth again, we may not know how we did what we did. But we have redefined ourselves in our own eyes and we are now a different person.

The 19th century author and physician, Oliver Wendell Holmes, noted that, "Man's mind, once stretched by a new idea, never regains its original dimensions." This includes our self-perception. Self-perception is just an idea we hold of ourselves. Once we perform at a level we didn't know was possible for us, we can never go back to that diminished sense of self that has limited us for far too long.

Have you ever seen a scared animal, tail tucked under, avoiding a confrontation? The old French word, *coart*, meant "one with a tail," and is the root of our word, *coward*. Cowardice is when we allow fear to keep us from taking action. It is the opposite of courage. Not the absence of fear, but the choice to act.

Once we act with courage, we know we can do it again. We have introduced a new level to our existence and to our self-understanding. When we act in cowardice, we stay captive in the grip of fear. But when we feel the fear and decide to respond with courage anyway, we become someone different.

Ordinary Heroics

As we've discussed, the challenges of our everyday lives and the repetition of our routines can lead us to operate on automatic. Doing the same things in the same way at more or less the same time, over and over and over again, can cause us to sleepwalk through life.

It sometimes takes life-threatening events to rouse us from complacency and inspire us to reorder our priorities. But what are our opportunities to act courageously in the course of our everyday lives?

Looking back again at the subjects we've covered in this book about how to thrive under all circumstances, we can see how they actually relate to courage.

For instance, **A Thought is Just a Thought**: when we give a thought power and it becomes a recurrent thought, it can gain the force of a commandment. And we all have those thoughts we tend to grab and nurture. They can come from lots of places. It is up to us to decide, though, that it is just a thought. They are just stories we keep telling.

And these stories can defeat us if/when we listen to them. They are often lies we tell ourselves about ourselves as lame attempts to account for our seeming flaws and failures. In truth, however, the path to success is always littered with failures. As Michael Jordan famously said:

"I've missed more than 9000 shots in my career. I've lost almost 300 games. Twenty-six times, I've been trusted to take the game winning shot and missed. I've failed over and over and over again in my life. And that is why I succeed."

What stands in the way of going for your dreams is often the belief that we don't deserve it, can't have it, or don't have the strength to do what it takes to make it happen. That's a heavy, disheartening barrage of negative thoughts to deal with. So, if you think it takes a lot of courage to fight an outer foe, just try standing up—and speaking back—to your own inner critic.

What you'll probably discover is a long lost part of yourself—the part that knows you can do whatever it is you set your mind to do. To remember, time and again, that "I don't have to believe everything that I think" is an act of courage that can ultimately help us turn our lives around.

It starts with courage to challenge the voices in our head that stand in the way of our greatness. This is what Thrivers challenge themselves to do on a regular basis.

Accepting What Is can feel like giving up. Yet, our natural tendency is to fight against what we do not like. However, if we have no direct and immediate means to alter what is happening, then the energy of opposition we expend in our resistance actually imprisons us.

It takes discernment to know when to resist and when to accept what is—and then courage to act on our choice. And there is no Right or Wrong answer. In fact, most often we need both acceptance *and* timely action.

When we are fighting against a moral injustice, we need all our energy to take courageous action. If we waste energy hating what's happening and blaming others for creating the problem, then we have less energy to do what needs to be done.

Forgiving Quickly and Moving Forward after we've been wronged is most definitely an act of courage and self-transcendence. When people have treated us unjustly, or caused us to suffer a great loss, and we don't forgive, the pain and rage can create wounds that last a lifetime. Better to come to acceptance of what has happened, to take full responsibility for the healing of our heart, and to let go of animosity toward the perpetrator. This all requires that we go beyond our instinctive, reactive behaviors into a place of forgiveness and greater peace. By doing so, we free ourselves from perpetual suffering. And in that freedom, we may even find a way to help other hearts, as well. Forgiving is a courageous action.

Showing Up—when all we want to do is disappear—takes both self-discipline and courage. Our habits, the repetitive routines of our lives, and the unpleasant situations we all have to face can really cause us to tune out and operate on automatic. Our minds tend to get stuck in the past and dread the future, rather than residing in this present moment where life is actually occurring. Thus, showing-up and being fully present to face whatever is going on in our life in the moment—whether it is tedious and dull, painful or embarrassing, or even the thrill of a lifetime—takes resolve and courage. But it's only when we do show up that we can live fully.

Taking 100% responsibility means taking ownership of whatever happens in your life—and that definitely takes courage to do. Our minds are so quick to point the finger of blame, to judge, and to find fault. It seems like a default setting to do just that. But ownership is not blame. Responsibility is choosing the direction, based on what happens.

Courage requires that we come out of our programmed reactions and behaviors into a greater state of awareness and responsibility. Rather than looking to see "Who did this to me?" we might ask a different question, like—"How did I get here?" This can then lead to further inquiries like, "What do I do now, given where I am?," ? "Have I let down my standards?," or "Why does this problem keep recurring in my life?"

It takes courage to question oneself in this way—and to be fully honest in our answers. But the payoff of bringing our unconscious behavior to our surface awareness is that then we can choose how we want to respond, rather than running on automatic. To act in accordance with our principles, rather than our conditioning, is essential if we wish to thrive.

It's easy to think that under ideal circumstances our behavior will be ideal. But what I have found is that by using the challenge of adverse circumstances to practice the tenets of thriving, we actually elevate our life condition in such a way that we are better able to endure the current circumstances and ultimately to move toward the preferred ones.

Exercising courage over the long haul—as a way of life—is hardly glamorous and rarely noticed. There are no badges and ribbons given to those who day-after-day, year-after-year, in every season of life, maintain the courage of their convictions.

The reward they reap by never giving up and never being defeated by anything—no matter what—is that they thrive! They develop an inner greatness that cannot be conferred by anything outside oneself—like fame, status, or wealth. Not even great accomplishment. Like courage, greatness is a quality of heart that is cultivated over time.

Why Is Courage Such a Necessity of Life?

Years ago I saw a cartoon in the *New Yorker* magazine in which a woman was sitting in front of her television set with a surprised look on her face. The voice coming out of the TV was that of an advertising announcer issuing this advice: "Ask your physician if taking a pill to solve all your problems is right for you."

Wouldn't it be great if such a pill existed? Imagine going through our lives without ever encountering a bump in the road. Life on "Easy Street." No struggles, no difficulties, no problems. Doesn't that sound appealing?

But then, what would we learn—and what would compel us to develop the courage and strength that our challenges call forth from deep within us? How would we discover the inner resources and capacities that we don't even know we have until and unless a problem greater than what we've known before necessitates that we do so?

Given that necessity is not only "the mother of invention," but also of personal development, the list of undesirable side effects for a pill that solves all our problems would have to say something like this, "Could induce a weakening in character, a lessening of motivation, a dulling of the desire to explore and to innovate, a deadening of conscience, and a laziness from which no good can come."

Looked upon from this light, our problems and challenges begin to appear like assets and blessings because they rouse us to action, promote a deeper level of self-awareness, and provide us with the opportunity to learn from experience. Only then can the wisdom that benefits succeeding generations possibly blossom and ripen within as we grow older.

It's easy to think that under ideal circumstances our behavior will be ideal. But what I have found is that by using the challenge of adverse circumstances to practice the tenets of Thriveology, we actually elevate our life condition in such a way that we are better able to endure the current circumstances and ultimately to attract the preferred ones. We have built ourselves sturdy, through our challenges, so we arrive at the place we want to be.

Courage—choosing to act courageously—is what builds our thriving muscles. When we take on challenges (courage), rather than stepping back from them (fear), we grow stronger. We thrive a bit more. We build more capacity to thrive in the face of the next life challenge.

TL;DR—Be Courageous

- Life is full of opportunities to act out of fear or out of courage. But fear and courage are not opposites. Courage is taking action, in spite of fear. It is not action in the absence of fear (that is just "action").

- Fears are a natural part of life. Our brains are super-sensitive to fear responses—originally designed as survival methods. Our ancestors were the more fearful who were more likely to live on the safe side, allowing them to have descendants. But those same fears that served well in the ancient savannahs and jungles now serve to keep us on high alert.

- We also have core fears that manifest our thoughts and hold us hostage. We all have some level of fear around three core existential issues:

  1. The fear of not having enough. Not based in truth, but in fear. Even those with plenty find it difficult to escape this fear

  2. The fear of not being good enough. Again, this is less based in truth than in a fear of inadequacy. It keeps many people chasing after attempts to prove they are good enough, and leaves others paralyzed from action, afraid to prove they are not good enough.

  3. The fear of not being loved enough. Humans are designed to be in community and connection with others. In fact, a high predictor of life satisfaction and health is the number of social supports a person has. This is the fear of not having those connections, of not being loved.

- A thriving life is a courageous life. It is courageous to "stare down" a thought, to accept what is, to forgive, to show up, to focus on gratitude, to seek purpose, to set and hold boundaries, to live to higher standards, to ensure you care for yourself, to connect with your spirituality, and to live your convictions. ALL require courage.

- When we act out of fear, we reinforce the fears. We give a bigger reality to that fear. The fear increases. When we act in spite of fear (with courage), the fear diminishes. We "starve" the fear and feed our thrive muscles.

- Acting on fear can be automatic. Acting out of courage is a choice.

Chapter 15

impact your world

"A life is not important except in the impact it has on other lives."
—Jackie Robinson

like it or not, all of us have an impact on each other—in big ways and small ways, both obviously and invisibly. There is no way around it.

Given this, Thrivers choose to go about their lives in ways that have a positive impact on the life all around them. And by so doing, they nourish and grow themselves. This is because acting with consciousness, kindness, and consideration for the Greater Good feeds our own heart and grows our courage. Conversely, having a negative impact on other beings (human and otherwise)—whether intentionally or inadvertently—in the long run erodes our own sense of self-worth, which can negatively impact our health.

It is easy to forget that we are interconnected on many levels. On a cellular level, each body is interconnected, with all the systems working together. As groups of people gather, first as family, then as community, then as nation, and then as world, we are all interconnected. And even with the rest of the natural world, we are interconnected. Any action we take on one level is felt profoundly through the rest.

Thriving is all about creating a positive impact on the systems, and throughout the world—no matter where we go. That's because thriving is an attitude and a practice that we cultivate daily wherever we are. It's what enables us to endure even the harshest, most painful circumstances.

We know this is true in large part because of what Dr. Viktor Frankl observed in the "laboratory" of a concentration camp. In such an unfathomable hell, those who found ways to have a positive impact on others fared far better than those who, quite understandably, succumbed to total despair. As Frankl pointed out, "Those who have a 'why' to live, can bear with almost any 'how'."

Frankl noted that the survivors were not necessarily the ones in the better physical condition. Instead, if an accident or intentional killing did not take them, those who survived were the ones who reached out to others. They were the ones that shared the last scraps of bread to feed another or who sought to relieve pain in another, trying to make the unbearable a bit more bearable.

Fortunately, most of us are never put to such a test. Our test is how well we can learn from the results of their test—and how we choose to apply what we learn with every choice that we make. Imagine how different the world would look today if leaders and citizens alike applied the wisdom in this statement, attributed to Peacemaker, Founder of the Iroquois Confederacy, circa 1000 AD.

"Think not forever of yourselves, O chiefs, nor of your own generation. Think of continuing generations of our families, think of our grandchildren and of those yet unborn, whose faces are coming from beneath the ground."

By considering not only our own needs and desires in the choices we make— but also the impact these choices will have on other people today and tomorrow— we have the power to create ripples of repercussions that can positively impact our world for generations to come.

Random Acts of Kindness

I believe that we are all designed to have a positive impact in the world—to live fully and to help others to do the same. Think again about the cells in your body. The overwhelming majority must be operating optimally for us to be able to thrive. Selfish cells are akin to cancer. Cancer cells do nothing actively to harm the system. They simply do not contribute to the health of the system. Over time, they take up more and more resources, giving nothing back in exchange. And over time, they crowd out the resources necessary to survive.

Today, the health and longevity of the world appear quite precarious. And many people feel there is nothing they can do to improve things. But what if all the individual selves in the world were convinced that they actually *could* make a positive difference, not only in their own lives, but also in the lives of their families and communities? Could the global malaise and decline be reversed?

We really don't know the answer to this question—Yet. But we do know that we can enrich ourselves and those around us in the process of finding out.

Of course, many throw their hands up in resignation and despair when hearing the news. They believe an ongoing decline in everything that is precious to us is inevitable. "What can be done?" they ask. "The problems are too widespread and overwhelming."

What these people often miss, however, is the fact that any change begins with the individual or a small group of individuals and spreads from there. The positive changes we make within ourselves—even if no one else knows about them—can still have a positive impact on others.

For instance, a friend of mine has a strong intention to show love wherever she goes. It's not something she talks about with many people but it is something she takes into her spiritual practice each day. And she doesn't do it to be a "do-gooder." She does it because it feels good!

At first, she was shocked when she heard some of the very words she used in her affirmations coming out of the mouths of strangers she encountered when they commented about her. For instance, one day in her morning practice she set the heart-felt intention to be a light in other people's lives. Then she went for a walk into town.

As she passed by a homeless man, he said to her, "Wow. Your smile just lights up my day." She was surprised and delighted by his comment and took pleasure in thinking about how the light he felt from her presence might assist him in his day.

What would happen if more and more people decided to run an experiment in which they took a few deep, healing breaths, centered their awareness on their hearts, and then set the intention to be their most beautiful self in the world in their interactions with other people? What kind of difference could that make if 10, 100, or 1000 people chose to do that?

The cultural anthropologist Margaret Mead stated, "Never doubt that a small group of thoughtful, committed citizens can change the world; indeed, it's the only thing that ever has."

Thrivers recognize the truth in this statement and the logic in the concept, "Think globally, act locally." By holding the intention to make a positive impact—right where we are—our acts of kindness and consideration spread like ripples on a pond. And they reach people at distances beyond what we'll ever know. Given how contagious a simple smile can be, a friend of mine likes to point out that the Miles in Smiles is an indication of how far we can reach and positively impact others when we offer a smile of kinship to a stranger.

Do you remember the phrase, "Practice random kindness and senseless acts of beauty"? The phrase occurred to one person, and ultimately changed the behavior of many people across the globe as it caught fire in the hearts of a few and then spread outward from there. For a period of time, strangers were behaving towards each other as people usually do *only* in times of disaster. And the ripple effect from that one phrase continues to reverberate around the world today.

Random Acting Out

If a system is designed for every part to work in harmony with every other—so that the "whole is greater than the sum of its parts"—imagine how some of those parts must feel if they're out of sync with the larger system. That's what happens to people who believe that there is no place for them in the world.

We all have times of not quite fitting in. We all have memories of feeling set aside, disregarded, ignored, and uninvited. The question is not whether these memories (just thoughts from the past brought into the present) exist, but whether we continue to allow them to shape our behavior and our choices. You WILL make an impact. Your option is whether that impact will be positive or not.

In order to Thrive, it's important to embrace your ability to have a positive impact in the world, knowing that your contribution makes a positive difference to the greater enterprise in which we're all engaged—whether it's a family, a classroom, a sports team, a committee, etc. If we view ourselves as unwanted and extraneous to others, how can we feel valuable to ourselves? Perceiving ourselves to be a "worthless" loner outside the circle of life can lead to very destructive behaviors—toward oneself and others.

This is because energy must have an outlet. If it finds no positive, creative outlet, it will find a negative, destructive one. All we have to do is glance at the headlines to see that this is true and to know the many forms that destructive behavior can take—including addiction to various harmful substances and practices, as well outwardly focused random acts of senseless brutality.

What a difference it can make when a helping hand is extended to an "at-risk outsider" at just the right moment. When such a person's inner value is reflected in the eyes of a respected individual— and opportunities are offered to cultivate their gifts and capabilities—then not just one life may be saved. The person who has been welcomed back into the "fold" may turn around and extend that welcoming invitation to others, thereby spreading the impact from that original act of kindness further and further.

I knew of a boy who grew up in the worst part of town. He was really struggling—failing in school and getting into fights and trouble all the time. It looked like there was no way he was going to escape poverty or live a meaningful life. A certain teacher took a special interest in this boy and began to nurture him and help him see his own potential.

The teacher tried to make sure that there were opportunities provided for this boy by the school. And once this boy felt that someone cared how well he did, he started doing a whole lot better. By high school, he was aware that he had something worthwhile to offer to the world. So he went on to college and prepared himself to make a significant contribution.

When I met him, I thought this young man would go into business, medicine, or the law. But he chose to become a schoolteacher. No doubt, he knew what a profound difference he could make in the lives of his students—based on how he turned his own life around when he met someone who saw his potential and wanted to help him actualize it.

Now, he works in an inner city school and one can only imagine how his deep empathy for his students' struggles inspires many of them to follow his lead and to actualize their own potential to make a positive difference in the world. Thus the impact of that one teacher, committing that initial act of kindness towards him, will likely create ripples for generations to come.

Points of Impact

Your place to begin is with you. Just as my friend's determination to be a beneficial presence in the world began in her own home and in her private time of thoughtful reflection, making an impact on our own body and mind is how we prepare ourselves to be able to make a positive difference in the lives of other people.

Self-Care: If you're taking care of yourself, and your intentions and actions are really geared to making improvements in your health and attitude, then your body can take you out into the world and enable you to achieve your greater goals. Conversely, if you're someone who wants to be of service in the world, but are struggling with your energy levels and health, then your potential for positive impact on others may be harder to fulfill. That's why self-care is so important. And given that we're all interconnected, when we challenge ourselves to do better than we have before—in body, mind and spirit—we may inspire others to take steps to live their lives more fully, as well.

Setting a positive example for our family will sooner or later exert a positive impact on them. This is especially true of our children. Our actions speak so much louder than words in influencing their values and character. Sometimes, it's just a matter of living out our thriving lives and sharing our experiences with them that ends up making the biggest impact.

From Self to Community Contribution: As I've already mentioned, at one point in my life I experienced a life-threatening health crisis. The perspective this gave me on my too sedentary lifestyle was a real wake-up call. I had allowed myself to get quite out of shape, which contributed to my falling ill. Once I recovered, I saw that I had a lot of work to do to bring my body back to full health and vitality.

I started working out at the gym and losing weight. People started noticing. Over time, I got into running, mountain biking, paddling, and other strenuous sports. I was inspired to get active by a friend of mine and followed his lead.

As I started looking and feeling far better, I noticed that my friends began to follow suit. It was like a ripple effect with expanding circles that embraced more and more people in my life—including my clients. People began to take better care of themselves through a variety of activities. I'd share the things that were working for me. And they would adopt some of those activities and tell me what other things were creating positive effects for them. At one point, I counted fifty different people whose lives were impacted by my resolution to take steps to get my body back in shape.

When a person is feeling healthy and strong, it's so much easier to contribute directly to the community. My own family joined the volunteer effort our church had been running for a number of years to feed the homeless. We saw that the need was great—not only among the homeless, but also with the volunteer program itself. So we wanted to be part of the solution.

Again, the ripple effect took over as more people from our associations, following our lead, joined in—and their friends participated with them. Then, members and their families from other churches joined with us. It became such a wonderful community activity that was inspiring to us all—and nurturing on many levels for the people to whom we offered food. They were touched and inspired by the pleasure they saw the volunteers having in the process of helping them out. What a teaching that is!

Anyone can start that kind of joyful ripple just by determining to make a positive difference in the lives of other people. You can start your own movement or join one that's already in motion. Just follow your heart—and many others will follow theirs in the same direction.

From Ripple to Snowball Effect

Fortunately, making a positive impact creates wider ripples than a negative impact does. More people are inspired to emulate acts of goodness than negative behaviors. And the more we act in positive ways, the more our acts impact us positively.

The more I got my body in shape, the better I felt. And the stronger I became, the more I felt like maintaining and increasing my nutritional and exercise programs. Seeing the impact this had on others caused me to desire to continue to work in all areas of my life to become my best and ever-better self. So being myself to the fullest became part of my sense of purpose, because I could clearly see how it influenced others to also be their own best selves.

Just look to the biographies of people who have had an extraordinarily positive impact on the world. It can be quite enlightening. We find that these were ordinary people—like us—and that they started small. They saw an injustice or some kind of problem or need that moved them to take steps to correct it. They didn't necessarily know where they were headed to begin with—or the impact they would eventually have. They simply took small steps in pursuit of their intention. And the impact these steps had on other people fueled their desire to keep on stepping out of their comfort zone and into the impact zone. It is in this way that our purpose unfolds.

Impact, and extraordinary change, come from ordinary people who act courageously, show up, reach out, and live out their own standards. We may see such people as extraordinary, but they rarely see themselves that way. Most great impactors only see themselves as a conduit for extending love into the world. They see an injustice and act with courage) to address it. They see a need and address it (high standards). They sense a prompting and refuse to let fear stop them. They choose to make a positive impact.

Don't wait to feel or be extraordinary. Who you are and where you are is enough. You already have it within you to make an impact. True impact comes from ordinary people acting on purpose, with courage, to make a difference. Look around you to see where you can make an impact now, not in some future place. You don't need more money, more time, more health, or more anything. You just need to bring your best self into the world.

Igniting the Fire Within

It is fear that keeps us playing small and stops us from being all that we can be. But what is it that we are afraid of? An answer to that question comes from Marianne Williamson in this insightful, now famous and highly popular statement:

"Our deepest fear is not that we are inadequate. Our deepest fear is that we are powerful beyond measure. It is our light, not our darkness that most frightens us. We ask ourselves, Who am I to be brilliant, gorgeous, talented, fabulous? Actually, who are you not to be? You are a child of God. Your playing small does not serve the world. There is nothing enlightened about shrinking so that other people won't feel insecure around you. We are all meant to shine, as children do. We were born to make manifest the glory of God that is within us. It's not just in some of us; it's in everyone. And as we let our own light shine, we unconsciously give other people permission to do the same. As we are liberated from our own fear, our presence automatically liberates others."

We all have greatness within us. All of us are capable of so much more than we even know. We have the power—and therefore the responsibility—to make a positive impact in the lives of those around us. And now that we are electronically connected with people everywhere, our decision to be our best self can make a wonderful difference in the lives of people we may never encounter face-to-face.

We're designed to live in ways that benefit more than ourselves. When we move in that direction we thrive. When we go in the opposite direction, we find ourselves in trouble. There really is no middle ground. Either we strive to make a positive difference in the world, or we become dulled by indifference, which can easily lead to lethargy, despair, and addiction.

Of course, the indifferent person may grow wealthy in money precisely because she or he doesn't take other people's needs into consideration. But the one who cares to contribute to other people's wellbeing grows wealthy in spirit—a priceless quality that takes time to develop.

All that's required of us to go from ordinary to extraordinary is the willingness to step beyond the fear and inertia, and to leave our comfort zone for the **impact**

zone. Whenever we find ourselves in the impact zone, we may feel the fears, but we also discover and live our purpose. We feel energized by our commitment and determination. Our negative thoughts cannot take control of us, because we're in action.

We've moved from that place of being held back by our limiting beliefs and misperceptions of reality to contributing to something greater than our little self. We're not out to "save the world"—or even to become more visible in the world. We're out to experience the pleasure that comes from having a positive impact on someone else's experience of life.

When we live like that, our intentions and efforts are certain to snowball. Whenever we take an action to fulfill a bigger purpose, it tends to grow, evolve, and expand. People around us get pulled into it. And as they join us in our project, the project itself gains its own momentum and has a growing impact we could never have imagined when we first began.

How to Become a Mover and Shaker

Wherever you are—and in whatever situation and condition you may be in at this very time—that's precisely the place for you to start. And the best time to start, of course, is *Now*.

Start with yourself, start simple and start small. Are there things you'd like to improve? If so, make a list and prioritize it—either by what needs to be done most urgently, or by what you can most easily persuade yourself to do on a consistent basis.

Focus on one area of your life and decide a few simple steps you can take to move yourself in the right direction. If your desire is to get in better physical shape, assess what your goals and needs are—in terms of nutrition and exercise. Then make a plan in which you start small and gradually increase your levels of whatever you feel you need to be doing. As each level starts to become routine, move it up another notch. Over time your efforts will become visible.

You can do the same with any area in life. Time to work on your boundaries? Make a list of the ways you have let your boundaries be crossed. Decide to strengthen your boundaries. Then, go and practice.

How about relationships? Perhaps you see some places where you can make a difference in how your relationships are going. Decide how you want the relationship to be, then look at your role in that. Decide to take responsibility to change that relationship. Begin moving in that direction.

This pattern of small and simple steps—taken one-by-one and worked into your routine—applies to whatever it is you want to do beyond what you're already doing. Make sure in the process that you're honoring your standards and your boundaries so that you stay on course with yourself.

As you raise your standards and performance level—with the determination to be your greater self—you will acquire a greater sense of meaning in life, because you're moving in the direction of your greater purpose. People will notice because you will be shifting energetically to a different level. Other people will move towards you, because they see the difference in your stature—in how you hold yourself—and in your influence on others.

Everybody loves a winner. And when you win out over yourself, people will want to know what you did and how you did it. Ultimately, everyone wants to be victorious and to be held in high regard. What becomes clear is that really, everyone loves a positive impactor—someone who sets out to make a difference. That's the win.

So start with yourself and your family and friends. Then watch your impact spread beyond the people closest to you in ways you could never have imagined when you first got it into your head that you deserve to be a person of influence around whom other people thrive.

Start small. Look for the little places to make a positive impact. The more you move towards impact, the more your life purpose will unfold. In the process, you may find yourself doing things you never envisioned, going deeper inside yourself, and experiencing a greater sense of value and meaning than ever before.

To get there, of course, we have to venture outside our comfort zone to arrive at the impact zone. And by taking small, progressive steps and actions—that's precisely the direction in which we'll move. We can never predict where the impact we make is going to take root. But we can be assured that when we set out to make a positive difference in the world, something of value will occur and our life condition will be improved in the process.

A little story: One morning, a man stepped out of his house, walked down the steps, and onto the beach. He wanted to see how much damage had been done by the strong storm that blew through the night before. Immediately, he could see the erosion all around.

He began strolling down the beach, enjoying the warm sun on his shoulders after such a powerful force as the storm had blotted it out the day before. The man was saddened by the damage, but had seen this before. He knew, soon enough, the beach would return to the gentle slope he loved so much.

As he walked along, he saw a small figure in the distance. He couldn't quite tell what the figure was doing, but it was a repetitive movement.

Walking closer, the man noticed a mass number of starfish that had been washed ashore during the storm, stranding them on the sand and drying them in the sun. "So sad," he thought. And he continued to walk toward the figure.

Soon, he could tell it was a small girl in her sundress. She was stooping over, standing up, and making a throwing action. Over and over and over she did the same action. And as he got closer, the man realized that she was gingerly scooping up the starfish and tossing them into the waves, just as the wave was receding, carrying the starfish to deeper water.

"Little girl, what are you doing?" he asked. She was intent on her action, and didn't seem to notice him. So he cleared his throat and asked again. "Little girl, what are you doing?"

She stopped, just for a moment, and said, "Saving the starfish," and just then, timed the next throw, tossing another starfish into the sea.

The man just stared as she continued.

"Why are you doing that?" he asked. "Because," the little girl said, not even looking at him as she tossed another starfish into the wave, "if I don't, they will die."

"But this is hopeless," he said.

She continued stooping down, tossing starfish after starfish into the sea.

"There are just too many," he said, "can't you see that this is hopeless?"

She continued. Starfish after starfish flung into the life-sustaining water.

"There are so many!" he exclaimed. "Don't you see? It doesn't matter. You can't save them all. It doesn't matter!"

The little girl, for the first time, looked up to the man, starfish in hand, and replied, "It matters to this one. . ." and stooped down to grab and throw another, "and to this one. . ." and she stooped again, "and to this one."

The man watched as she continued her efforts. Then, he slowly stooped over, scooped up a starfish, and gingerly tossed it into the ocean. Then he grabbed another, tossing it. And another. And another. Each time, he thought "and to this one, and to this one."

What is YOUR impact? Where is YOUR impact zone?

TL;DR—Impact Your World

- We all impact the world. The question is whether we impact it in a positive or a negative way, and whether we are conscious or not of our impact. For example, research is very clear that parents have a huge impact on their children. Yet many parents forget this fact and fail to notice the impact (positive and negative) they are having on a child (and future adult).

- Any impact we make in the world has a "ripple effect." It triggers others to make other impacts. This is true, whether the impact is positive or negative. An adult who mistreats others was often mistreated as a child. The impact continues. A child who is loved has the capacity of loving, which then has a ripple effect.

- Positive impact is rooted in a sense of meaning and purpose. When people have lost a sense of meaning, when there is no sense of purpose, it is less likely that an impact will be positive.

- Thrivers understand the ripple effect of how they impact the world. They seek to create a positive impact. Doing so also brings a deeper sense of meaning and purpose. This creates a powerful cycle of bigger impact, deeper meaning and purpose, bigger impact, and even deeper meaning and purpose.

- Start the impact with yourself. Start with self-care, so that you have the strength and capacity to carry an impact into the world around you. Small impacts begin to grow, when they are consciously carried out.

Chapter 16

grow

thriving people are growing people. Their education doesn't stop with graduation, but is on-going throughout their lives. People who thrive challenge themselves regularly to step out of their comfort zone and develop new capacities for exploration, adaptation, and enjoyment of our ever-changing world.

Thriving is not about arriving at some final destination where, at last, we are complete: We have reached our goals and can now simply sit back and enjoy our life from here on out. The truth is, in this perpetually spinning, rapidly changing world, once we stop growing—we start dying.

You've no doubt played with a spinning top and noticed how it starts to wobble when it begins running out of energy. We do, too, when we decide we've somehow "arrived"—we have what we want, we know enough, we have done enough, exercised enough, and now it's time to just "kick-back" and enjoy life. The only problem is that once we stop advancing, we start retreating.

How many people have we heard of who worked for decades at some job or other, then finally retired with high expectations of basking in their golden years?

Unfortunately, as soon as there was no longer any incentive for them to keep moving ahead, like the tired top they toppled over.

We're all programmed to grow. It's built into our DNA. We start out microscopically small in our mother's womb, then grow up to be people who can have a major impact on the world. When growth and change stop, life begins to fall apart.

Do you remember learning about entropy in physics class? It's the tendency for systems to fall into disarray over time, unless new energy is put into that system. As soon as I learned about entropy as a teenager, I put it to immediate use as an explanation for the mess in my bedroom. My parents appreciated my new knowledge, of course, but not the mess. So, the excuse never got me very far. Still, the understanding of entropy—and how this tendency can affect us all—really stuck with me.

Entropy is the latent possibility in anything. It's part of the cycle of birth, aging, sickness, and death. In order for us to maintain a state of aliveness throughout our whole life, we need to keep growing in every area of life, throughout life.

Of course, we're not going to grow taller after we reach maturity. In fact, we might even grow shorter in our later years (and perhaps heavier). But one of the ways we *can* maintain our physical stature and delay the onset of entropy is by staying active and exercising regularly. We also have to continue developing our minds and all our capacities in order to live with vitality.

In truth, it's "not really over until it's over." Up until the time they wheel us away, we're charged with making the very best of our life because it's the only one we have—whether we dwell in a castle or a hovel. And it's by taking a growth orientation toward life that we're able to make it worth living. In the inimitable words of Jimmy Buffett, "I'd rather die while I'm living than live while I'm dead."

Old Dogs & New Tricks

Most people underestimate their capacity for creativity, learning, and change, and that's part of what leads to their reaching a place where they just stop growing. Up until recently, it was generally believed that our genetics were responsible for everything, that our personality was set in early childhood, and that our brains couldn't change past a certain age. Now we know—from recent research in neuroscience—that these old assumptions, which were long considered fact, are actually fallacious. Just look at how many "old dogs" are using technology and learning about the vast world of cyberspace.

The brain turns out to be very "plastic." Research shows that even when people are injured by an accident or a stroke, their brain can rewire itself and new capacities can emerge. It may be more of a challenge to learn when we no longer have the nimble brain of our youth. But challenge is what we're all built to take on.

I have a friend whose mother lived by that principle. She earned a Master's degree in early childhood education in her late fifties and built her own highly successful nursery school. In her 70's, though she already spoke French and Spanish fairly well (in addition to her native English), she taught herself the rudiments of Hebrew, Greek, and Italian, so she could read the writers she admired in their original language. At 80, she enrolled in the local community college to develop her artistic abilities.

In addition to refreshing her drawing and painting skills, she studied conceptual art and computer graphics, purchasing a Mac desktop computer and a large color printer so she could share her creations. Her son was a composer, and a musician friend of his commissioned her to design his album cover. She would have kept on going with all her creating and growing if cancer hadn't overtaken her. Just before she died, close to her 89th birthday, she remarked to a friend, "I've turned into an old woman in just these last two weeks."

As my friend's mother demonstrated, people late in life can still master foreign languages and modern technology. The secret of this woman's success may well have been that she approached everything she was interested in with the curiosity of an eager child who believed in her own capacities. She had a playful spirit and enjoyed the challenge of allowing her curiosity to lead her to new places. Struggle was never part of the equation for her. She was just having fun.

We really don't know the extent of our abilities until necessity—or curiosity—compels us to stretch in a whole new direction. It might feel uncomfortable at first, but expanding our comfort zone usually does. And on the other side of it lies a whole new territory that rewards our perseverance and awaits our exploration.

Necessity can force our hands. Changes in health or career can lead to re-toolings that were not desired nor pursued. But even change that is based in necessity must be accepted and chosen. Many people can be in the same situation and simply refuse. But then they are stuck with the results their resistance creates.

Curiosity creates a chosen course of change and growth. Curiosity is one of those traits of a natural thriver, always seeking out a new vista. The natural thriver finds engagement in the possibility of growth and in the possibility of exploration. And curiosity provides a softer avenue for growth than does necessity. But in either, one must still choose to grow and develop beyond the here and now.

Late Bloomers

There are many people who say, "You know, after a certain age, it's all down hill from there." That's a great excuse for "retiring" in front of the television set or behind a computer screen. But it happens not to be true—unless you commit yourself to making it true.

Research shows that even seniors who decide to get into shape can do so. Their bodies will respond. So, it's not just the brain but the body, as well, that can learn "new tricks" at any age. In fact, a man who grew up in a family of aerialists had a student who began taking classes with him in flying on the trapeze in her 70's.

There are also the legendary Tarahumara people of northwestern Mexico. They are renowned runners who can traverse great distances across difficult terrain. And they are said to become even better runners later in their lives.

There are many examples in the world of people who, later in life, decided to take on something new and made a success of it. They may have started new businesses, began writing books, become visual artists, or any of a number of things.

One outstanding example of a late bloomer is Ray Kroc, who turned McDonald's into the most successful fast-food franchise in the world. Up until the time he started working with the McDonald brothers, he'd held a number of positions including jazz musician, pianist/band member, salesman, and radio station DJ. He joined the brothers in his early 50s and didn't buy them out until ten years later.

A question he would ask that has inspired me for years is this: "Are you green and growing or ripe and rotting?" Those are our only two options. To grow requires that we continually find ways to develop ourselves—up until the very end.

Julia Child didn't even know she had a real taste or talent for cooking until she was in her mid-forties. She described her first dinner in Rouen, France to the *New York Times* as an "opening up of the soul and spirit for me." So much of our soul and spirit remain a mystery to us until we are prompted by curiosity or necessity to seek to discover our latent interests.

Anna Mary Robertson Moses, better known as Grandma Moses, is another famous example. She decided to devote herself to painting at age 78 and achieved great renown after that. What she left behind are the nostalgic, colorful impressions of a simpler, more peaceful time in American history, which you've no doubt seen on greeting cards, calendars, etc.—especially around the Holidays. What she also left behind is a reminder that we never have a legitimate excuse— short of debilitating illness—to grow old.

Experiments have been conducted demonstrating that our beliefs of what old age looks like, in terms of progressive biological deterioration, really are just that: beliefs. Change your beliefs and you change your results—including blood pressure, bone density, and other standard measures of aging.

Our life-long capacity for discovery and learning is key to a thriving life. There are so many shortcuts presented to us in the popular media for how to get happy quickly. But I think the real shortcut to a thriving life is not short at all. It's a lifetime of constantly exploring and expanding into new areas of interest and service. Think what a service Grandma Moses did for so many by doing what she'd always wanted to do.

Staying Open to All Possibilities

Carol Dweck, Ph.D, is one of my favorite authors. She explains how, like the set of a sail, our mindset determines our direction in life. According to Dweck, there really are only two kinds of mindset: a fixed mindset and a growth mindset. Can you imagine trying to sail a boat any distance without being able to shift the sail with the wind?

Dweck states on her web site, "I have always been deeply moved by outstanding achievement, and saddened by wasted potential." Whether we believe it and can see it or not, we each are laden with the potential to do extraordinary things. If we have a fixed mindset, and believe that one has to be "naturally gifted" in order to excel, then we will stay fixed in place, unable to satisfy deeper yearnings within our being for greater self-expression and contribution. A fixed mindset leaves us believing that there is an inborn talent that we do not have that prevents us from being capable in ways we would like.

With a growth mindset, we understand that no matter where we are in our life in this moment, we can always move ahead in the direction of our dreams. And with consistent effort, we can attain satisfying results. Capability is built through learning and practicing.

All of us have places where we get stuck and places where we give ourselves room to grow. When we're operating from a fixed mindset, we are prone to think, "This is how it is and it can't get any better. I might as well accept it and move on." Or even worse, "Why even try? I just don't have that ability/gene/capability/discipline."

When we are operating from a growth mindset, our inner dialogue sounds more like this: "How can I grow into something new? How can I develop some new skill? How can I develop some new understanding? How can I continue to grow into the person that I believe I was designed to be?" If we wish to thrive in this life, we can adopt and nurture a growth mindset—even in the face of inner or outer voices of opposition.

I'm convinced—in fact, I absolutely know—that our mindset is more important than our physical abilities and talents when it comes to fulfilling our potential to live a thriving life. Have you seen the amazing 2005 documentary, *Emmanuel's Gift?* It's about a young Ghanaian man, Emmanuel Ofuso Yeboah, who was born with a severely deformed leg. That's a death sentence for most babies in Ghana, or a life sentence of begging on the street for handouts from a disdainful public.

When Emmanuel was growing up, there were no social services, education, or employment for deformed people, as they were believed to be cursed by God. Feeling shamed by having fathered such a child, Emmanuel's father abandoned the family. But his mother devoted herself to nurturing and educating him. Emmanuel then took it upon himself to demonstrate that handicapped people are no less capable than others.

The film details what he accomplished, and the undefeatable spirit with which he did it. His efforts attracted international allies and led to great improvements in the lives of many people in his country. I highly recommend you watch this inspirational documentary as it will help you release all excuses for not doing whatever you have to in order to actualize your amazing potential to live a thriving life that benefits many.

Another extraordinary man with everything going against him is Nick Vujicic. Born with tetra-amelia syndrome, Nick is one of seven people in the world without arms or legs. As you can imagine (or can you?), he is a motivational speaker capable of inspiring large audiences of ordinary people to do extraordinary things.

Letting Go of Ever Arriving

As far as I can tell, life is not about getting somewhere. It's a process of becoming more and more of who we are, at deeper levels of our being.

Most people have a dream of what life will be like when they reach a certain level of achievement in their personal and/or professional lives. But what often happens when the day arrives—and life goes on—is that this feeling doesn't last. It turns out that the real joy comes from setting, then striving, to reach important goals that are always a little beyond what we currently think we can do.

Looking forward to new possibilities in life—rather than backward with regret at missed opportunities—is a defining mindset for those who Thrive. So is enjoying the journey's ups and downs. Many who have been working hard to arrive at a particular destination find themselves quite bored and unhappy once they actually do. Often, what's most important is what happens to us and how we change, grow, and learn in the process.

Many successful people I've spoken to—regardless of whether their success is in their personal or professional lives, or both—have openly shared with me about the many humbling stumbles they experienced all along the way. They all confided that the journey was painful at times but that the payoff was worth the price.

Those I've worked with who are struggling to create a successful marriage are often held back by the fact that they are focusing on the past rather than on new or latent possibilities. When we have a growth mentality and believe that things can change for the better, then we're less likely to get stuck looking at what has already happened.

The past has passed. It does not exist any more. Yes, there are lingering residues (thoughts and beliefs)—in terms of feelings and the repercussions from choices made. But all of these can be managed if we maintain a growth mindset and seek to use every experience as a learning experience from which we can discover how to do better next time. Whenever we say, "Well, I can't get there, because look at where I've been," we close off all the possibilities for ourselves. And, we overlook all the other people who have been in similar or even worse places yet found a way to grow around these places --even because of them.

Whenever we find ourselves in a place of being stuck and feeling stagnant and unhappy, it's time to ask ourselves, "What needs to change here? What's my next point of growth along the path?" Often, the place to start is in our attitude and outlook.

The World Opens Itself to the Curious

Children are naturally curious. The newer they are, the more the world excites their interest. Take them to a museum or just watch them in your own backyard. The smallest crawling creature will fascinate them as much as the enormous bones of dinosaurs. They have an insatiable need to explore their world and to know how and why things are the way they are.

The idea that "curiosity killed the cat" is clearly absurd (and, by the way, a misquote). What "kills" our interests is boredom—which is totally unnecessary. Unfortunately, at times, we may just stick to our routines and repeat our habits while feeling increasingly disenchanted with life.

When we reignite our curiosity, we become once again more vitally interested in life. And that's when our awareness of our own capacities also wakes up—because we've allowed ourselves to stretch beyond the boundaries of our customary way of being. Curiosity is what stretches us. It stretches us into new places of interest, discovery, and possible accomplishment.

When people come into my office and say, "I just don't know what to do next," I have a simple suggestion for them: Walk into a bookstore and just start perusing the magazine covers for images and articles of interest. Maybe it's something that's been outside their realm of development up until now. But if they find themselves drawn to it, it's certainly worth exploring.

Here's a fact you might find especially interesting and maybe even a little intriguing: Often, the way a field of study advances is through someone from outside the field exploring it with new eyes and without the encumbrances of old theories and beliefs. Who knows what you may discover just by allowing yourself to explore interests you may have forgotten you ever had.

What are you curious about and how can you light the fires of your curiosity to ignite a new passion for living? One of the places I would like to suggest is that you become more curious about yourself. What really makes you tick—and why? What impact are you having on your world and what impact would you like to be having? How can you get free of the past events and find a place of greater peace and self-acceptance inside yourself? Where do you go from here? And what have you always wanted to do but never thought you could?

When we ask ourselves such questions, we awaken that inborn sense of curiosity that can lead us in unexpected directions. We may end up developing interests and capacities we never even imagined that we had. But, how enriching they are to our life and possibly to the lives of others. Tapping into our natural sense of curiosity brings forth new things, simply by noting the curiosity that is already there.

Learning from Our Challenges

When challenging events in life happen, I do not believe it's because the Universe sent them to teach us a lesson. However, I do believe that there are lessons that can be learned from any situation—whether it's something that thrills or saddens us.

When we make our life a laboratory of learning, then we learn how to expand ourselves and uncover hidden capacities to meet whatever situations manifest in our lives. As the famous 19th Century German philosopher, author, scholar, and composer Friedrich Nietzsche famously believed, "That which does not kill us makes us stronger."

When a challenge comes along, if it doesn't do us in, it provides us with profound learning opportunities. But we have to be willing to look for the lessons rather than being stuck in a victim mode. It's by taking 100% responsibility for our lives that we are able to find other ways of being in the world through discerning and learning all that we can from whatever occurs.

When we take a learning attitude toward life, we look for the gift in every hardship. We ask ourselves, "What does this have to teach me? How can I learn from this? How can I apply it in my life?" We may not see the value in this approach in the moment we're really struggling with a challenge. But over time it will become more clear.

As Steve Jobs pointed out, it's always easier to connect the dots looking backward than looking forward, so you may not know where it's going to land you. But there are lessons to be learned and places to be stretched and curiosities to be nurtured all throughout our lives. All we have to do is start with a desire to see what else there might be for us in life.

Life is all about growth. We are either green and growing or ripe and rotting. The challenge each one of us faces through life is how to stay vital, alive, and growing up to the very last breath we take.

TL;DR—Grow

- Thrivers know that growth is a lifetime endeavor. Others believe that growing is over at some point in life. They believe that children grow, but adults don't. But thrivers know that the course of life is always about growing and changing. It is about challenging yourself, stretching yourself, and taking on new challenges as they arrive.

- Life is constantly offering opportunities for growth and change. When we ignore those opportunities, they don't go away. They return over and over. We either grow through them or find ourselves constrained by them.

- A "Growth Mindset" (as noted by Carol Dweck) is the mindset that we can always learn and grow. A "Fixed Mindset" is the belief that abilities are genetic and pre-set. When someone is seen as a "natural" athlete, writer, mathematician, or any other title, this comes from a fixed mindset. The fixed mindset limits people by creating the illusion that "you either have it or you don't." This leaves people unwilling to try something new. If someone has been assigned a "natural" ability, they can either work their entire lives to prove it or not disprove it.

- Those who adopt a growth mindset believe that they can grow and learn, improving over time with practice and deeper understanding.

- Being "in process" is thriving. "Arriving" usually leaves us stuck. And the key between the two is often curiosity—to see what else is possible, what else is out there, what else is awaiting.

- Life is an endless creator of challenges. Life doesn't do things to us. But as life happens, there are challenges. Embedded in every challenge, every struggle, is the opportunity for growth. All that is required is a growth mentality.

Chapter 17

conclusion

When I was a teenager, I had an interest in magic. It taught me many lessons in life. I probably learned more about perceptions and psychology from doing magic tricks (and fooling people) than any graduate class ever taught me.

I also learned about learning. One summer, we had been on vacation and on the last day, I bought a magic trick at the magic store (my favorite hangout at the time). This trick was not a complicated trick. But I had imagined all sorts of special machinations in the little wand that was part of the trick.

Thinking it would be a great new trick, I grabbed that trick on the way out of town, knowing it would be an easy learn on the ride home.

I was wrong. The little wand had no special mechanisms. It was a trick based on a sleight-of-hand. One I did not know. And by the time I realized it, there was no turning back to talk with the shop owner.

For the life of me, in that hot backseat, I could NOT get the sleight to work. My hands would not do it. I tried. I tried again. I tried again. I grew frustrated. I put it down and swore it didn't work.

But it was a long trip. After a while, my pouting didn't get me anywhere, so I decided to try again. I failed again. And I tried again. And again. And again.

I put it down, swore I would never do it again. And then I grew bored. With nothing else to do, I tried again. And again. And again.

Then, at some point, my fingers pretty sore from trying the same little move over and over, it worked! I suddenly had it. I could do the move.

I went from not being able to do it, swearing it could not be done, to being able to do it.

Until my muscles finally figured it out, learning was about trying.

When I was performing, I also learned about fear. My mind, before every show, would tell me how dangerous it was to perform. What if people laughed at me (or didn't laugh when I wanted them to)? What if the trick failed and they figured it out?

Sometime along the way, I forgot what to say, said it wrong, or messed up a trick. And you know what? My guess is that nobody remembers that. Or even remembered it an hour after my performance. In fact, I realized that my fears were in my head. Every audience was cheering me on, hoping I would succeed and not fail.

And there is one other lesson: things are always more simple than we make them. People would often try to tell me how I did a trick. And they were (almost) always wrong. They came up with very complex and complicated ways that something happened. They never guessed correctly because they always made it more complicated than it could ever be.

I feel that way about thriving in life. We just make it so complicated. We assume all the things that need to be in place before we can "be happy" (I hope that by now, your goal is to thrive and not just to "be happy").

And interestingly, we also have a tendency to make it too easy. We see a meme on the internet, a pithy quote, and believe it should be easy. And then we believe it must be easy for other people.

In reality, thriving is simple. It is not easy. Thriving has some skills, as we have covered. And we do have to put in the effort to learn and implement the skills. But the skills are straightforward and simple. That still does not mean easy.

Habits and old ways of being don't go away without a fight. Even if those "ways of being" are no longer effective, we tend to hold onto them. It is often based on automatic ways of reacting. Usually, those patterns of behavior worked for us at one time. Otherwise, they wouldn't have developed. But now, those behaviors no longer work.

Still, it takes time and effort to get ahead of them, to set them aside and move forward. Which is simple. But not easy.

Control What You CAN Control

We have several arenas over which we have control. We have several areas over which we cannot control. Part of thriving is making sure you are focused on the right targets, taking control where you can, and accepting the areas you cannot control.

You cannot control Fears and Feelings. But you can choose your Aspirations, Attitudes, and Actions.

Fears are automatic. As we have noted throughout this book, fears come upon us. They are a natural occurrence based on the fact that we are wired to look for threats. There is no way we can stop the fears. They pop up when we least expect or want them. And the triggers are just about impossible to stop.

It may be a tone, a look, an expression, from somebody. It might be a dark building or a letter in the mail. The triggers are endless. And immediately, the body goes on heightened alert. Fears just come upon you.

Being gripped by fear, though, is different than allowing that fear to determine your actions. You do have a choice in how you respond to those fears. Will the fears shut you down or simply alert you? Will the fear be an Avoidance Indicator or an Importance Indicator?

You also do not have control over your feelings. The feelings and emotions you have are just the feelings and emotions you have. They are neither right nor wrong. They simply are what you are feeling.

Many times, people feel bad about the emotions and feelings they experience. Yet they have no way to stop those feelings. And the more focused they become on those emotions, the more entrenched those emotions become.

Yet, one step back are the thoughts. As we demonstrated earlier, those feelings are the result of the thoughts you hold onto. When we grab onto a thought, turn it over, examine it, build it up, and believe it, the feelings follow. While you cannot control the feelings and emotions, you do have a choice on how long you choose to hold onto a thought. A thought is just a thought.

So, what CAN you control?

Aspirations. Your aspirations are the opposite of your fears. In fact, what you fear usually has a corresponding aspiration. They reside down in your core beliefs. For example, someone who fears a disconnected marriage (showing an importance associated) has an aspiration for a connected and loving marriage.

Or someone who has a fear of speaking in public often has an aspiration to share something important. The two go hand-in-hand. The size of a fear of anything is usually in proportion to how important it is to you. And if it is important to you, it is connected to an aspiration you have.

You get to choose your aspiration. You can choose the aspiration to follow, to feed, to develop. Your aspirations lead you in the direction of your purpose and your impact. Aspirations call forth your best self. So, you show up, you raise your standards, and you set your boundaries.

Aspirations are the starting point, not the end point. If you merely have aspirations, but don't move toward them, you just have a dream. Dreams are fine. But they don't lead much to thriving. There must be more.

Attitudes. Sometimes, people have an aspiration, but repeatedly tell themselves that "I can't do that," or "Why do I deserve that," or "I may as well give up now." That is the attitude. It's your outlook.

Do you focus on a "Can-Do" attitude, or a defeatist attitude? As my scuba instructor (and now friend) said at the outset, "Choose a positive mental attitude." This is a choice you can always make.

As Henry Ford long ago noted, "Whether you think you can or think you can't—you are right."

Many times, the difference between moving forward and staying stuck is having an attitude of potential and of focus. Choosing one's attitude is an important skill. Otherwise, we assume that an attitude is automatic, and not within our choice. Attitude is always a choice, when one decides it is.

Thriving is not for the few or the fortunate. It is not just a matter of good fortune (or even great fortune). Thriving is not reserved for the people who won the genetic lottery, born to the wealthy or powerful. Instead, thriving is in the reach of every person.

On our default settings, we often allow ourselves to be pulled into fear, blame, and avoidance. That is just the ruminations of our brain and our culture. We live in a world, with a brain, built to focus on survival. Getting by. Avoiding trouble.

Ironically, that only leads to trouble. And it keeps us playing small in life. Suddenly, the "easy" path is not so easy. The "survival path" keeps people just hanging on, hoping for more, but without pushing for more.

The "thriving path" is not so much fighting instinct, as it is recognizing that we often misuse the clues of life. When fear pops up, we let fear dictate our reactions, rather than allowing fear to point us toward the important.

When tough times hit, we avoid and blame, simply because we don't see the opportunity for growth that is embedded in the challenge. Tough times are the training grounds for greater growth and a bigger life.

Choosing A Thriving Path

On default, we can get stuck in "survival mode." It is our base setting. This is what keeps us alive and moving. But it is not a mode that allows for optimal living. It is just about "living." And that mode has been developed over the millennia of human development. It was designed for a much more primitive and threatening world.

Now, we have greater and greater opportunities to do something different, something more. We can choose a "thrival mode," a life of thriving. But we must choose it. We have to make a conscious choice to step forward, beyond survival, to a thriving place.

The choice to thrive is the starting point. Making a conscious decision to move forward begins the process. From there, it is simply a matter of skill acquisition and thought shifting.

You are here because you want to build a more thriving life. Quite simply, you would not have chosen to read this, unless you did. And quite simply, if you have arrived at this point in the book, you have more than a passing interest. You have begun to build a more and more thriving life.

Have you noticed a shift in your thinking, a change in your direction, as you moved through this book? Have you gain new skills and understanding? Have you noticed a difference in how you respond to events in your life?

You are now further down the road of building a thriving life.

That is a journey that will last the rest of your life. And the beginning point was simply a choice to move in that direction. In that instant, you chose to take responsibility for where you are headed, for how you will live your life.

As you move forward, continue to work the 15 Thrive Principles. When you find yourself dropping back to your default Survival Mode, remind yourself of the principles. The chapter summaries will serve as a great "kick-start" to get you moving in a thriving direction again.

And remember to join the Thrive Nation here:

http://Thriveology.com/book

A free eBook edition is available with the purchase of this book.

To claim your free eBook edition:

1. Download the Shelfie app.
2. Write your name in upper case in the box.
3. Use the Shelfie app to submit a photo.
4. Download your eBook to any device.

Shelfie

A free eBook edition is available
with the purchase of this print book.

CLEARLY PRINT YOUR NAME ABOVE IN UPPER CASE

Instructions to claim your free eBook edition:
1. Download the Shelfie app for Android or iOS
2. Write your name in **UPPER CASE** above
3. Use the Shelfie app to submit a photo
4. Download your eBook to any device

Print & Digital Together Forever.

Snap a photo   Free eBook   Read anywhere

The Morgan James
Speakers Group

www.TheMorganJamesSpeakersGroup.com

We connect Morgan James published
authors with live and online events
and audiences whom will benefit
from their expertise.

Printed in the USA
CPSIA information can be obtained
at www.ICGtesting.com
JSHW022320140824
68134JS00019B/1203